WHO
DO YOU THINK YOU ARE?™

WHO
DO YOU THINK YOU ARE? ™

THE GENEALOGY HANDBOOK

THE ESSENTIAL POCKET GUIDE TO
TRACING YOUR FAMILY HISTORY

DAN WADDELL

BBC
BOOKS

1 3 5 7 9 10 8 6 4 2

Published in 2014 by BBC Books, an imprint of Ebury Publishing.

This edition published 2018

A Random House Group Company.

The Random House Group Limited Reg. No. 954009

Addresses for companies within the Random House Group can be found at
www.randomhouse.co.ukThis edition published 2018

A CIP catalogue record for this book is available from the British Library.

ISBN: 978 1 78594 342 3

Penguin Random House is committed to a sustainable future for
our business, our readers and our planet. This book is made from
Forest Stewardship Council® certified paper.

Printed and bound in Great Britain by Clays Ltd, St Ives plc

Commissioning Editor: Lorna Russell
Project Editor: Louise McKeever
Copy-editor: Sarah Chatwin
Picture Researcher: Victoria Hall
Design: Two Associates

Who Do You Think You Are? is produced by Wall To Wall Media Limited, which
is part of the Shed Media Group Limited.
Genealogists: Sara Khan, Laura Berry
Series Producer: Kathryn Taylor
Executive Producer: Colette Flight

Who Do You Think You Are? name and logo are trademarks of Wall To Wall
Media Limited and are reproduced under licence.

To buy books by your favourite authors and register for offers visit
www.randomhouse.co.uk

Contents

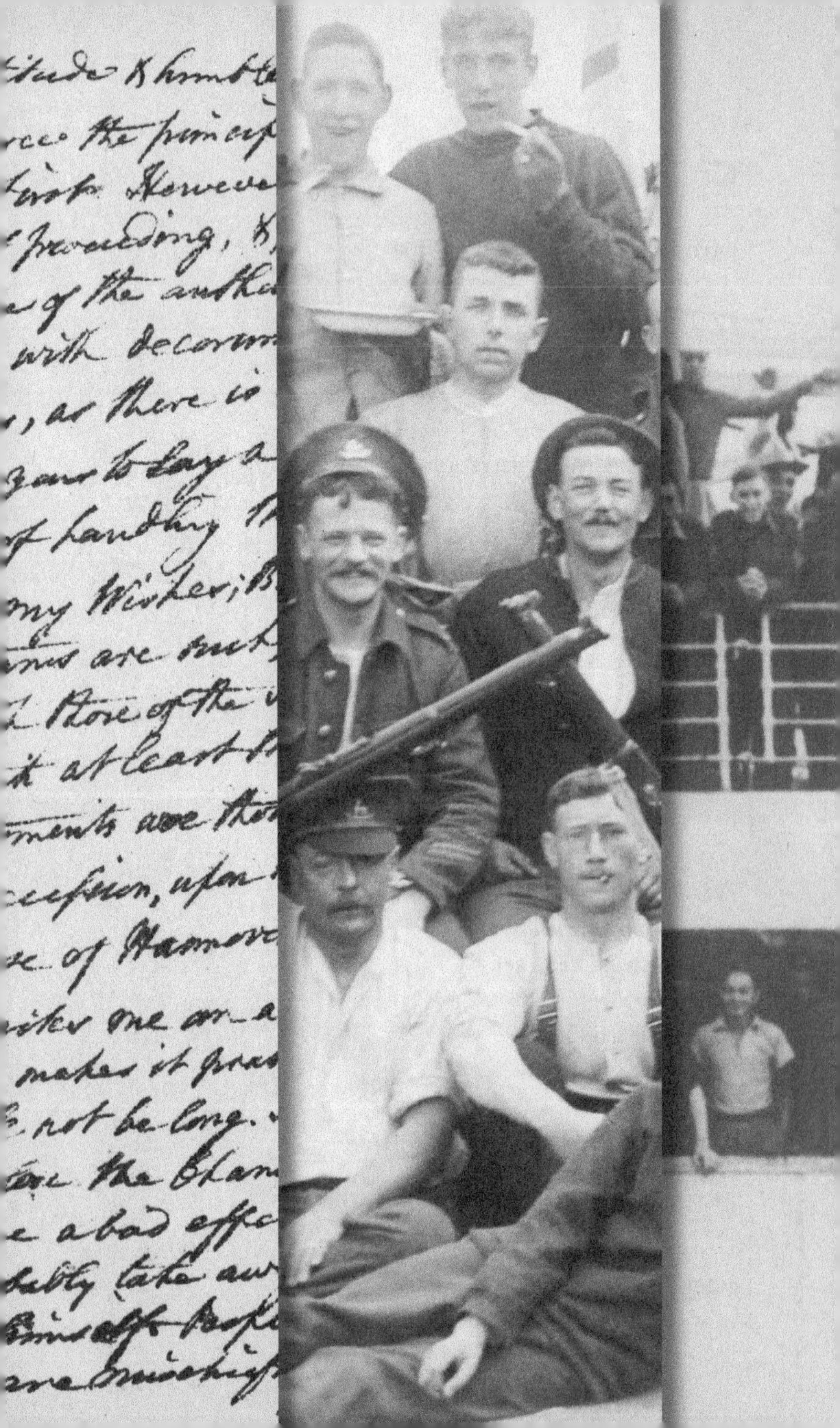

INTRODUCTION

In 1988, television producer Alex Graham settled down one Sunday morning to read the newspapers. He came across an interview with fellow Scot Billy Connolly in which the comedian spoke honestly and movingly of his family history. It occurred to Alex that while Billy was an international star, his family's story of working-class hardship and struggle was shared by millions of other Britons. He had the idea of a series of programmes where well-known people told their family history.

* * *

He pitched the idea to the BBC but they turned it down. For 15 years it languished in the bottom drawer of his desk at Wall to Wall, an independent production company, until Jane Root of BBC TWO visited the company looking for ideas. The channel was still basking in the glow of successful programmes like *Great Britons and Restoration*, which had proved that TV shows about history could attract healthy viewing figures. Alex and his team decided to re-pitch their celebrity genealogy idea, now tentatively titled 'Back to My Roots'. This time the BBC were interested and the series, to Alex's delight, was commissioned.

But then the hard work really started. For a few weeks the team thought they had bitten off more than they could chew. Persuading ten celebrities to appear on a show which would dig into their past – possibly revealing unknown secrets – without finding out a single detail until the cameras started to roll, proved to be an enormous challenge. Undaunted, they drew up a list of around 200 celebrities, researched their ancestry and targeted the best stories. Many refused, but Alex and his team persisted.

The first celebrity to agree was Bill Oddie. His involvement not only gave the series (its title by now changed to *Who Do You Think You Are?*) its first subject, but also changed the format. Until that point the intention of Alex and his team had been to use the celebrities to illustrate ten major stories and events from British history, such as the Industrial Revolution, the First World War and the Irish Potato Famine. But Bill told them he was less interested in his family's role in the rise and fall of the cotton industry during the Industrial Revolution than he was in the story of his mother, whom he'd never really known. Throughout his childhood she had been in and out of hospital, and no one had told him what was wrong with her. It was that story which fascinated and motivated him.

It presented Wall to Wall with a dilemma. Should they defy Bill and risk him pulling out by telling him they were only interested in his family's role in the Industrial Revolution? Or should they go along with his request to investigate his mother's illness? Wisely, they chose the latter, and the template for future episodes was set. The series would try and tell an alternative British history by highlighting major themes in our island's story, but it would also follow the subjects on an emotional journey into their past. It is this combined appeal, of bringing history to life and following someone on a personal quest, which has created the show's enduring popularity.

The first episode aired on 12 October 2004 to record viewing figures for BBC TWO. Now, ten years after that first episode, *Who Do You Think You Are?* has marked its 11th series and its 100th episode. There have been books, DVDS, live events and the format has been sold to more than 20 different territories. In that decade it has covered a vast range of themes: tales of immigration and emigration, struggle, tragedy and hope, lives lived in illness, crime and poverty, and war stories. There have been tears of joy, anger and sadness. Without exception, each celebrity has found something new and surprising on their journey, a revelation that has given them greater understanding of their predecessors and, in some cases, their own lives.

The scale of the show's success still surprises Alex. 'The most gratifying thing is the love people have for the show and the intensity of that love. I've been fortunate to have been involved with three or four programmes that have "crossed over" and connected with people, and *Who Do You Think You Are?* is probably most prominent among them.'

More of us than ever are going back to our roots. There are many reasons for this, of which the success of *Who Do You Think You Are?* is one. Another major factor is the increasing amount of information available online. Meanwhile, growing numbers of us have discovered that tracing our family history is not just a trawl through endless archives, but an addictive and emotional journey into our pasts. Often we don't know where our research will take us or what we might find. An unclaimed legacy or a secret royal link are unlikely, but there's a good chance there's a war hero or a black sheep waiting to be discovered. This process of revelation is what makes it so addictive. For many of us it will be the closest we come to detective work – interviewing people, following clues, solving puzzles, overcoming dead ends, until we get to the truth.

This guide will equip you with the basic skills to make that journey. It will give you some tips about putting flesh on those bare bones, so you are not just able to find basic information about your ancestors but the circumstances in which they lived and the lives they led.

Happy hunting.

John Willcox

m. E.

William

m.

Hannah

oseph   Henry

m. 1842

n Davis

(widow) b c1811

James   Willia

c1849

Susan b 1847   Chas. Henry

ifford

Park Bristol

He

GETTING
STARTED

GETTING STARTED

The most difficult step in family history is the initial one. The flow of accessible information from archives to Internet has become a torrent and there are a bewildering number of websites offering all kinds of information. So much so that people often wonder where to start or how to navigate through the mass of available material. But the old adage remains true: in order to trace the dead, the best place to start is the living.

* * *

The simple fact is that if you're lucky enough to have surviving relatives from a previous generation, whether that's parents or grandparents, then you have the perfect starting point (if you don't, never fear; the next section has a short guide on how to get started by putting yourself first). Not only will a chat with them yield precious nuggets of information to kick-start your quest, it's also an ideal way to preserve an oral history of your family. In an increasingly fractured world, where instant communication is king, and our eyes are fixed firmly on the future, we are losing precious chances to record the past and the memories of those who lived through it. It's a great idea, with their agreement, to record interviews with any relatives. Not only does it free you to listen carefully to what they're saying rather than having to scribble down notes, but those tapes or files can be used by your descendants when their time comes to research their pasts. If your relatives live a long distance away and you are not meeting them face-to-face, make sure you type or write up the notes of phone conversations as quickly as possible afterwards while your memory is still fresh, or print out an email chain if you've done the interview electronically. There are also ways of recording conversations over the Internet too, using programmes such as Skype. It's well worth the effort. The same goes for keeping any photographs, diaries, letters and other mementos you might collect. Your children or nieces and nephews might not seem too interested now, but there will come a time when they will want to know more about their family and their place in history.

Before you start interviewing, write down everything you know (or think you know) about your family history. Include any family stories or legends. Sketch out a rough family tree if possible. At this stage it might only feature you and your immediate family but it will indicate where the gaps are and where you should target your research. Put yourself and your immediate family at the centre of this tree with any dates of births, marriages and deaths you know, the names and details of any siblings, your parents' names and significant dates if possible, as well as any other relatives. It doesn't matter if this is just a rough diagram at this stage. There's no need to invest in an expensive piece of genealogy software just yet. There are templates you can find online, or you can even do it yourself with a piece of paper and a pencil. Put your generation's branch at the bottom of the page, then your father and mother's name above that, if known, and each of their parents' names above that and so on. However, it's entirely up to you how you structure it, or even if you structure it all. The only 'must' is that you find a method to organize your research for easy reference as you proceed.

It is also worth asking whether anyone else in your immediate or distant family has drawn up a family tree. If so, try and get hold of a copy. It can save you a lot of work – although, of course, it's worth double-checking the dates and names are all correct. Kevin Whateley's brother Frank had a family tree that their father had put together more than 50 years before, which set the actor on a journey

John Willcose (carpenter
m. Elizabeth   di___

George   William (bd Aug. 10/1819
                                m.
                                Hannah (" May 3/185?
                                        b 177? Bl___
Field Farm (1871 census)

___ary ___   John   Joseph   Henry   Isaac
B. Witchel   m.   m. ___1852   m.
b 179?   Mary Tillett Ann Davis   Elizabeth
Yatton Kennett   (widow) b ___1811   Sherbo___
Lived at
2? Farm House
Stoke Gifford (1881 census)

                                        James   William   Alfred
                                        ___1845   ___1852

        Sidney ___   Richard   Susan b 1842   Chas. Henry b 1847
        Benjamin   Bennett
        b 1835   b 1387? Stoke Gifford
        m.,
        Emma Willcose
                          (1901 Living 1st Elgin Park Bristol)

                                                        Henry   Edith
        Richard Sidney b 1890   b 1866   b 1873
        m.   (Bristol)
        Marjorie Cullen   ??? ???
                                                        1st w__?

John   Jean   1871 C___

...ford, Som.)
...809,

Hester
m.
William Williams

Mary
m.
James Collins

Benjamin
Living with mother
in 1851 in Stoke Orford
Both born in Barrow, Som

Hannah

Lucy

Sa...
Geo. Lu...

Ellen

Hannah
1858

Annie 1867
m.
Samuel Davis
b 1834
Iron founder
Salts

Emma
m.
Sidney B...

2nd marriage
Davies in 1861
Census

(children...

...hel A
1875

Mary E
b 1878

Horace E
b 1880

Bruce

The Davis Family Tree

15

Sidney B Whitehall — Barlee Farm

back into the eighteenth century to unearth a story of wealth and religion. A family tree can help you pinpoint and focus your search on the ancestors that interest you most.

Armed with the bare bones of a family tree, and with a note of any family stories, it is time to arrange and prepare for any family interviews. Here are a few tips to bear in mind:

- **BE FLEXIBLE:** Write down any questions you might want to ask beforehand, but don't be a slave to them. If the interview veers off in unexpected but interesting directions, then you might learn more. You can always return to your list later in the interview.
- **BE RESPECTFUL:** If you're recording the interview, whether it's in person or over the Internet or phone, you should always tell your interviewees and make sure they're comfortable with it.
- **BE ENCOURAGING:** Keep your questions 'open-ended'. Questions such as 'What do you remember of your childhood?' will elicit more information than 'Do you remember your childhood?' and encourage your subject to open up.
- **BE PATIENT:** Memories can be hazy and people need time to recall events. There's nothing to be gained by subjecting them to a Jeremy Paxman-style interrogation! Allow your subjects to speak and minimize any interruptions to avoid derailing their train of thought.
- **BE SENSITIVE:** All families have their secrets, and some people are not willing to speak about them. Respect people's privacy and their feelings and steer clear of contentious subjects.
- **BE VIGILANT:** Don't accept everything you are told as gospel truth. All families have their myths that turn out to be untrue, and all of us are prone to lapses in memory. If possible, cross-reference information with other family members. I was once

told a distant relative was killed in the American Civil War. It
turned out to be nonsense.

These interviews are also the perfect time to collect or copy
any photographs, documents or memorabilia your subject has.
Comedian Rory Bremner's quest to know more about the military
deeds of his father, who died of cancer when Rory was 18, first took
him to his brother Nigel, who had inherited the family archive.
Among the photographs and other memorabilia, he found a letter
that confirmed his dad had seen front-line action in the Second
World War and indicated where. This offered priceless detail which
not only brought his father to life, but also gave Rory a starting place
for his research.

At the top of any wish list should be birth, marriage or death
certificates, which are the building blocks of family history research.
Diaries and letters contain information that can aid your search,
but they also offer a fascinating insight into the lives and times of
your ancestors.

Family photographs are manna from heaven because every
picture tells a story. There's an immense power in staring at photos
of people long dead, and also a kick in working out from whom you
inherited some physical traits. It's always a good idea to check the
back of photographs to see if someone has written the date on which
it was taken, even the names of those featured. If there's no date,
look carefully at what people are wearing because clothes can offer a
clue to when it was taken: for example, in the late Victorian period,
women's dresses were often simple and plain, while earlier on in
Victoria's reign they were often adorned with ribbons and bows.
If the men are in military uniform, buttons, medals, caps or insignias
can indicate their regiment or rank. Other heirlooms include war

Circa 1895: Several generations of a Victorian family pose for a photograph in their garden.

or service medals, often inscribed with regiment or ship names, or press cuttings about significant moments in your ancestors' lives, or even their own deeds.

Whatever you collect, make sure you store it carefully. Old photographs are very sensitive to light and heat or damp, and need to be kept somewhere dark, cool and dry. A shoebox makes an excellent storage facility, and also allows easy access when you need to refer to its contents.

Once you have completed your interviews, and collected all the materials and heirlooms you can possibly find, it is time to ask yourself exactly what the aim of your research is. In most episodes of *Who Do You Think You Are?*, the featured celebrity is interviewed at the start of their journey and indicates what they're keen to find out. Bill Oddie, as we mentioned, was keen to know the truth about his mother's illness. Go through your notes and see if there's a story you want to look into first. Of course, as has happened in the show many times, your research might take you down another path entirely, but a clear idea of what you want to know can help to focus your research. Perhaps you want to discover whether Uncle Bill really was a serial bigamist, or find out more about the mysterious case of Auntie Doreen and her missing husbands...

If you don't have a clear goal in mind and just want to trace your family's path from the past to the present, like many people do, then it is best to choose one branch of the family to research first, to avoid being overwhelmed. You'll have your surname, probably passed down by your father, and your mother's maiden name, which opens up another branch of investigation. If you have the details of your grandparents, then that's another four names and maiden names to research. If you're aware of who your great-grandparents are, then that's another eight names and before you know it things can get extremely confusing and complicated.

Pick a branch and go as far as you can with it, then return to the start and investigate another branch. Many people begin with their father's family because that's the strand that gave them their surname, but equally many others start with their mother's. If you have no preference, the key for beginners is to select the side of the family that's easiest to research, which means the branch with the most distinctive surname. The rarer a name is, the easier it is to trace. So, if you're someone who's been teased for having an unusual surname, this is where you can have the last laugh: the long-suffering Shufflebottom family will find it much easier to trace their lineage than the boring old Smiths!

What's in a Name?

We can learn a lot about our ancestry and roots from our surnames. Much of it will depend on where your family came from, but if your ancestry is British, many names can be separated into four main categories:

- **PLACE NAMES:** Some of the most common surnames originated from a desire to differentiate people according to where they lived, often a small local landmark. So John who lived near the hill was known as John Hill, and John who lived beside the village green became John Green. Other common surnames of this type include Brook, Beck or Moore (from Old English meaning 'open land' or 'bog'.)

- **PATRONYMICS:** Many surnames derive from the name of a father in the mists of time – such as Johnson, Robertson, Jackson (son of John, Robert and Jack, respectively) – which has then been passed down the line. Fascinatingly, in Iceland this traditional practice still continues. If Jon Siggurson has a son named Olafur, he doesn't become Olafur Siggurson but Olafur Jonsson (i.e. the son of Jon).

It applies to daughters too, so if Jon has a daughter named Birna, she becomes Birna Jonsdottir.

- **OCCUPATIONAL:** Back in feudal England, there was a need to differentiate between John the Blacksmith and John the Wheelwright, so they became known as John Smith and John Wright, respectively. Many of our most common surnames are derived from this source: Baker, Taylor (from tailor), Cook, Cooper (a craftsman in wood) and Miller, for example.

- **NICKNAMES:** There is a sense that all surnames are nicknames because they were given to people so as to be able to differentiate them from others. But this specific type of surname was given to people because of their looks (common terms you may come across: dark and swarthy and they might be called 'Black', while the pale-skinned might be named 'White'), stature ('Short') or physical traits ('Strong' is self-explanatory, but 'Ball' might be given to someone who was short and fat). Finally, and most intriguingly, there are those who were named for their habits. 'Fairweather' might be someone of a sunny temperament, whereas 'Moody' might mean exactly that. It's not always literal; the surname 'Drinkwater' could mean your ancestors liked to drink water, or it might have been awarded sarcastically because they were drunks who might be better off drinking water!

BILLY CONNOLLY

A CASE STUDY

It's appropriate that the comedian Billy Connolly should feature in the series in which *Who Do You Think You Are?* celebrates its 100th episode. More than a quarter of a century ago, it was his story in a Sunday magazine which inspired Wall to Wall founder Alex Graham to come up with the idea for a genealogy series involving celebrities. Here, thanks to Producer Anna Kirkwood, of Wall to Wall, we show how his absorbing story was pieced together using civil records, parish registers, census returns and military records.

Billy grew up in Anderston, a working-class district of Glasgow. His mother left when he was just four years old and Billy became close to his maternal grandmother, Florence McGowan. At the outset, his aim was to learn more about her roots. He was also hoping to discover an ancestor whose wild behaviour he might approve of!

Scottish Ancestors

At the start the team were optimistic they would be able to track Billy's Scottish roots fairly swiftly because Scottish birth, marriage and death records are generally more detailed than their English counterparts. For example, a Scottish marriage record will contain the maiden name of the mother of both bride and the groom. Likewise a Scottish death record gives the names of both parents of the deceased, including the maiden surname of the mother, and a Scottish birth record provides the dates of the parents' marriage. One of the best online sources for Scottish research is Scotland's People, a combined project of the Scottish National Archive and the Scottish General Register Office. It provides access to records of probate, parish registers and census returns. But, as it turned out, Billy's story took a different turn and he wouldn't be searching Scottish records for long.

Billy's search started with his grandmother Florence McGowan's birth certificate, which revealed she was born in 1902 to Patrick McGowan and Mary McGowan, née Doyle. Using this information he was able to find eight-year-old Florence living with her parents on the 1911 census. Mary and Patrick were both recorded as having been born in Lanark, east of Glasgow. Billy had previously believed that his great-grandparents were Irish immigrants. Perhaps it was the generation before who came from Ireland? Tracing further back, Billy located Patrick and Mary McGowan in the 1901 census. However, this census stated that Mary was born in Ireland. A mystery! Where was Mary born? Ireland or Scotland?

Discrepancies in the Records

Census returns are a fruitful resource for genealogists. But, like all records, they can be subject to discrepancies and inaccuracies. As today, the census was compiled from forms filled out by every householder in the country and collected by an enumerator. In times of high illiteracy, some people needed the help of neighbours and others to fill out the forms. Therefore it is not uncommon for there to be inconsistencies in the spelling of names, dates and locations of birth, etc. Be wary of taking the results of a census at face value. If any obvious anomalies crop up between returns it's worth exploring because they can be the clue that leads to an entirely new family history.

Research failed to uncover a birth record for Mary Doyle in, Scotland, Ireland or England. Instead, to Billy's astonishment, a baptism record revealed that Mary had been born in Bangalore, India! The baptism also provided the names of Mary's parents – Margaret and Daniel Doyle – and, crucially, gave Daniel's occupation as a gunner in the Royal Horse Artillery.

Military Ancestors

The National Archives in Kew hold a vast array of military
records, including records for soldiers who served in the
British Army. It is helpful to know whether your ancestor
was an officer or a private, as this will dictate which set of
records to search. If, like Daniel, they were a private, the
first thing to look for is a service discharge record. These
records of service survive if a soldier was discharged and
awarded a pension. They can provide key biographical
details, such as where your ancestor was born, their
occupation before military service, and even a physical
description. If you know the regiment your ancestor
served in then you can also search for them in muster
rolls and potentially medal rolls.

Daniel Doyle's service record didn't disappoint. Billy discovered his
Irish connection – Daniel came from Hollywood, County Wicklow,
Ireland, and enlisted in 1856, aged just 18, before travelling to India
as part of the 3rd Battalion 60th Rifles. Though Daniel arrived in
India during the 1857 Indian Rebellion, he didn't see any action
because he was stationed in the south, while most of the fighting
occurred in the north. The service record also revealed that he was
awarded three good-conduct badges and was promoted to corporal
in 1863. But he was no model soldier – he appeared 16 times in the
regimental defaulter's book. The diary of another soldier in the Royal
Horse Artillery provided a rich description of the boredom that

afflicted soldiers like Daniel in peacetime, which frequently led to misbehaviour. Billy's suspicions that drink might have been part of Daniel's downfall proved to be founded. His army medical record disclosed that he was suffering from alcoholism, and later, syphilis. Billy had certainly found his wild ancestor - 'a real Jack the Lad'.

But Daniel Doyle isn't the only military man in Billy's family tree. Daniel married Margaret O'Brien in India in 1869 and her baptism named her father as John O'Brien. John's occupation was given as 'Private 1st M.F.', which meant that he was part of the first Madras Fusiliers at the height of the Indian Rebellion. A medal roll revealed that in 1857 John was part of the force sent to relieve Lucknow, where 2,000 British soldiers and civilians were barricaded in the British residency as protection against the attacking rebels. After a gruelling journey in which they suffered heavy casualties, John and his fellow soldiers finally reached Lucknow, where they, too, became trapped inside the residency. A Madras army register revealed that John O'Brien suffered seven gunshot wounds to his shoulder during this campaign, the reason why he left the army and was pensioned off shortly afterwards.

Anglo-Indian Ancestry?

Margaret O'Brien's baptism record from 1852 revealed that she was born to John O'Brien and Matilda Allen in Bellary, India. Billy had now uncovered two generations of his family born in India. But what about the generation before that? Margaret's father was John O'Brien of Irish origin, but what about Matilda? What was Matilda doing in India and what could Billy find out about her roots?

In his quest to find out more, Billy searched the church records at St Patrick's in Bangalore, one of the main Catholic churches in the city, where he was able to find a marriage for John O'Brien and Matilda on 16 July 1845. Disappointingly, the record didn't contain any information about Matilda's parents, but searching the baptisms turned up a tantalizing clue: Matilda's baptism recorded that she became a Catholic on 20 May 1845, just weeks before she married John O'Brien. Even more surprisingly, it revealed that Matilda was only 13 when she married John. Why was Matilda so young when she married? The answer was in the marriage record for John and Matilda's daughter, Mary. Mary was recorded as 'East Indian', meaning Anglo Indian. Billy was delighted to discover this meant that Mary's father (John O'Brien) was European, but her mother, Billy's 3x great-grandmother Matilda Allen, was Indian!

JERRY SPRINGER

Television presenter Jerry Springer's first memory was of sailing into New York past the Statue of Liberty in 1949, aged five. With him and his sister Evelyn were his father, Richard, and mother, Margot, a couple who had fled Nazi Germany on the eve of the Second World War and sought sanctuary in England during the war, before emigrating to the United States. Jerry knew 'bits and pieces' of his ancestors' story, but like many Jews who managed to escape the horror of the Holocaust, recalling the time before their lives were destroyed and uprooted was often too painful.

THE START of his emotional journey, which would become one of the most moving episodes of *Who Do You Think You Are?*, was his birthplace: London. He learned from the Association of Jewish Refugees that his parents were among the lucky 80,000 Jewish refugees whose lives were saved by England's willingness to increase the number of refugees it was prepared to offer safe haven, while nations such as the USA stuck to a quota.

* * *

From there he sought more answers, in particular why his father had been forced to leave his home and thriving shoe shop in Landsberg (now Gorzow in Poland, but then part of Germany) in 1937. In the town's archives he learned that the small, wealthy Jewish community had been subject to persistent anti-Semitic abuse following Hitler's rise to power in 1933. Unable to stomach any more persecution, they fled their small town in favour of the capital, Berlin, believing that safety might come in numbers.

It did not. His parents escaped weeks before Hitler invaded Poland and war started, among the last Jews to make it out of Germany. Others were not so fortunate, including his widowed maternal and paternal grandmothers, Marie Kallman and Selma Springer. Jerry knew they became victims of the most unspeakable atrocity of modern times but he wanted to learn their exact fate.

He learned Marie was transported to a Jewish ghetto in Lodz, Poland, where this proud, well-to-do woman of 64 was forced to

Jerry's maternal grandmother,
Marie Kallman.

share a single room with five others without furniture, beds or
proper sanitation. Six months later she and thousands of others
were forced into cattle trucks and deported by train to Chelmo
concentration camp. There, Jerry stood on the site where she and her
fellow deportees, oblivious to their fate, were told to strip to bathe
and led onto 'gas vans' – the precursors of the gas chambers that
would follow – and murdered.

Returning to Berlin, at the Potsdam Archive Jerry was shown documents that proved that Selma, together with her brother Hermann, were 'resettled' in Theresienstadt, another Jewish ghetto. German propaganda portrayed it as a pleasant retirement community, but in reality it was a squalid, desperate place rife with disease, overcrowding and starvation. Of the 140,000 Jews sent there, 130,000 would die. Among them was Selma, who died in the ghetto hospital, aged 72. It was little comfort, but at least Jerry knew she was spared the awful indignities and terrors of transportation to Auschwitz and the gas chambers.

Jerry had reached the end of an almost unbearably poignant journey into one of history's most shameful periods. But his grief was lifted somewhat when he was introduced to a relative from a branch of the Springer family he never knew existed, whose ancestors had also managed to escape the Holocaust and settled in Israel. It was a reminder that even in the bleakest, most horrific circumstances, families can endure. 'Hold on to your family,' Jerry said. 'It's all you really have. There'll always be someone who continues.'

Selma Springer, Jerry's paternal grandmother.

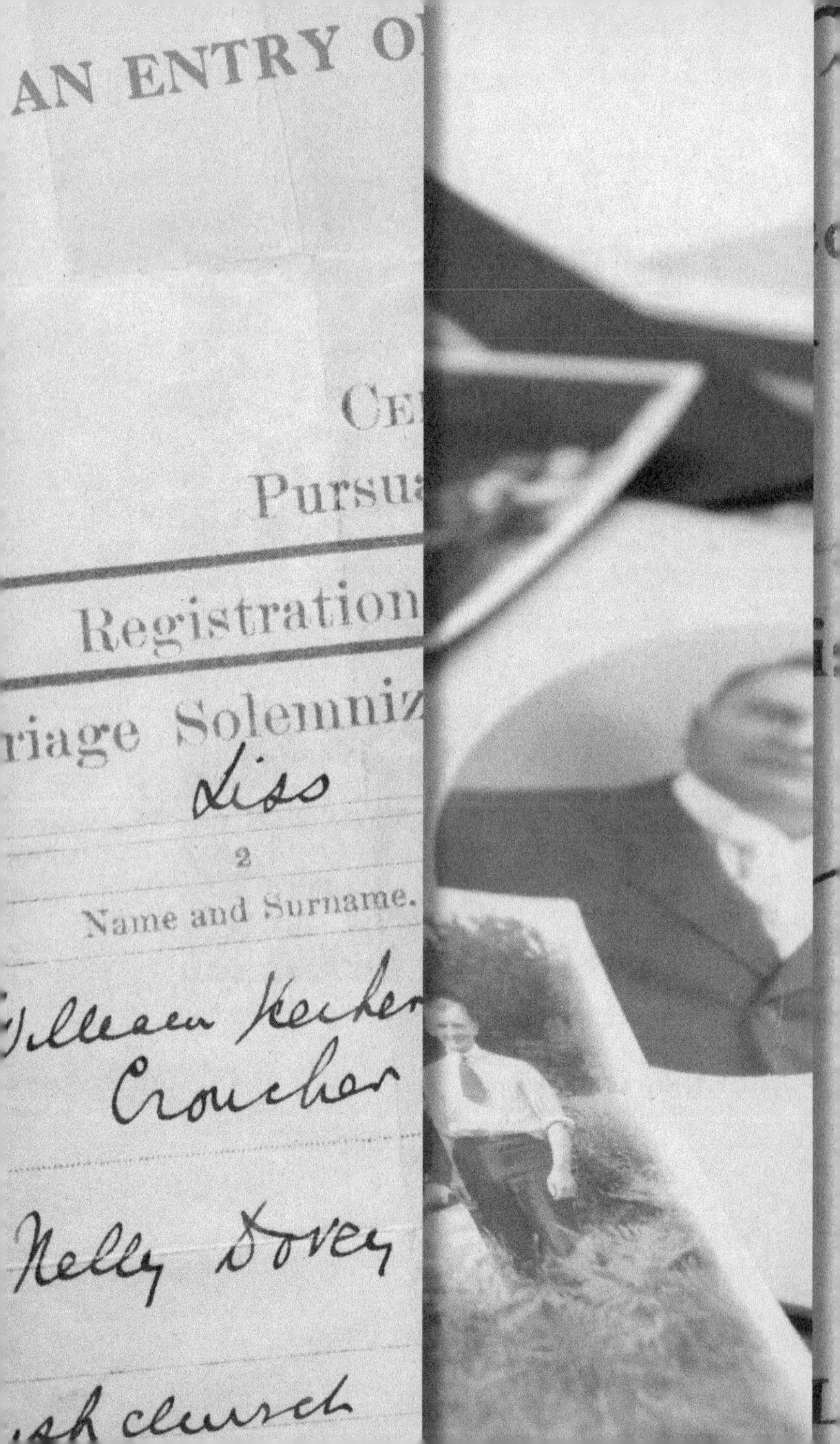

CE

Pursua

Registration

rriage Solemniz

Liss

2

Name and Surname.

William Kerker
Croucher

Nelly Dovey

sh church

ify, That
of *Willia*
his Wif
was
of
Hore
. in the
at whose

FIRST STEPS

Civil Registration
Records

ry, Redcross

FIRST STEPS
Civil Registration Records

Everyone who was born or married or who died in the UK in the modern era has left a trace of their existence. Exactly how much of an imprint they made on history depends on their wealth, social standing, occupation and exploits, as well as a series of other factors. But even the lowliest will have left a mark if they lived after 1837, which is when the era of civil registration began in this country, and people were required to register births, marriages and deaths. These certificates, which can be located in indexes for each year since, are the building blocks of family history and they are crucial to your search.

* * *

Prior to 1837, there was no national registration scheme. By law all christenings, weddings and burials were carried out by the Church of England, and recorded in Parish Registers (which we will examine later). But these records were often patchy and incomplete, while the growth of 'nonconformist' churches and groups meant that some people's entire existence went unrecorded altogether. By compelling citizens (although it only became a legal requirement after 1875) to record their journey from cradle to grave with the state, ostensibly to monitor population growth and trends more effectively, the government of that time did future genealogists of all kinds a gigantic favour.

That doesn't mean that some people didn't slip through the net, but they are incredibly few. Some people recoiled in horror at the prospect of being 'monitored' by the state and refused to divulge information, risking punishment, while others gave false details for the same reason. As you search through the indexes and registers for an elusive ancestor, it may be that you can't find any evidence of his or her existence. Such problems are common; however, the trick is not to panic and assume your ancestor went unrecorded. There is likely to be a far more innocent explanation.

It might be a case of misspelling. Your surname might not always have been spelled the way it is now. At various points in my family history the name Waddell was spelled Weddle, Waddle and, on one particularly hard-to-find certificate, Wardell. This was because many of my ancestors were simple coal-mining folk and were unable to read or write. As the registrar wasn't told how to spell it, he or she would have guessed or written the name phonetically and, given that my ancestors were from Scotland and the northeast of England, with their own accents and intonations, it would have provided a challenge! Before you set off on your quest it is worthwhile to consider your own surname and contemplate any other ways it could be spelled. For example, if your ancestor's surname started with 'H', then bear in mind it might have been dropped in telling, and so the 'Hanson' family might occasionally have been recorded as 'Anson' and so on.

What Can I Discover?

Birth Certificates
Birth certificates are a wonderful source of information. They provide details that enable you to find marriage certificates, which can be used to find more birth certificates and so on. Reading the form from left to right, this is what you can find:

F. No. 4058   D

THESE are to certify, That *Florence* *Daughter* of *William Edward Nightingale* and *Frances* his Wife, who was Daughter of *Wm Smith Esq. M.P* was Born in

in the Parish of

in the City of *Florence* the *twelfth* Day of *May* in the Year *eighteen hundred and twenty* at whose Birth we were present.

Frances Gale

Frances Lombard

57

Registered at Dr. WILLIAMS's Library, *Redcross Street*, near *Cripplegate, London*. *July 12th 1820 Thos. Morgan* Registrar.

Florence Nightingale's birth certificate, 1820.

- **WHERE AND WHEN:** your ancestor was born. The first main column will give you the precise date and location of their birth.

- **HIS OR HER NAME:** This will be the full given name, including any middle names, which is very useful for cross-referencing with census returns and other sources of information. Occasionally parents had not decided on a name within the six-week registration period (which is why the column is headed 'Name, if any').

- **FATHER'S NAME:** First name and surname of the father.

- **MOTHER'S NAME AND MAIDEN NAME:** The maiden name is a priceless piece of genealogical information, allowing you to trace the maternal line further back by finding the couple's marriage certificate, a birth certificate for the mother and so on.

- **FATHER'S JOB:** Another invaluable snippet. Knowing an

ancestor's occupation allows you to work out his or her social rank and status, as well as opening up the possibility of searching employment records to find out more about them.

- **FATHER OR MOTHER'S SIGNATURE AND ADDRESS:**
Here's a chance to see your ancestor's signature, although, due to high levels of illiteracy in the past, sometimes you might see a cross or mark instead of a signature. Genealogically speaking, the address is more important because it's another piece of information to use as a cross-reference and can be very useful when used alongside census returns.

The rest of the form is less useful, giving the date of register and the name and signature of the registrar.

Marriage Certificates

Marriage certificates are another indispensable genealogical source. They provide information about those related to the newlyweds which can open whole new avenues of research. Here's what the form can tell you:

- **RELIGION:** The section across the top of the form will tell you where the marriage was performed, usually a church, which can indicate which religion your ancestors followed, as well as the district or parish.
- **DATE OF MARRIAGE:** The exact date on which your ancestors were married.
- **THEIR NAMES:** The full names of bride and groom, including middle names.
- **AGES:** This might seem straightforward but it often isn't. Sometimes people lied about their age, particularly if there was a rather large age gap between them and their spouse! Don't be shocked if you have ancestors who married at 14 or 15 here too.

No.	When Married.	Name and Surname.	Age.	Condition.	Rank or P
117	12th September 1846	Robert Browning Elizabeth Barrett Moulton Barrett	Of Full age	Bachelor Spinster	Gen

1846 Marriage solemnized at *the Parish Church* in the *Paris*

Married in the *Parish church* according to the Rites and Ceremonies of the

This Marriage was solemnized between us, *Robert Browning* ... In the Presence of us,

*12th September 1846: The marraige certificate of
Roberst Browning and Elizabeth Barrett registered
at St Marylebone Parish Church, London*

Before 1929, when it was raised to 16, the age of consent was 14
for boys and 12 for girls. Learning your ancestors' ages allows you
to find their birth certificates (as long as they were truthful...)

- **CONDITION:** No, this doesn't mean how fit or otherwise
  they were. It states whether the person getting married was a
  bachelor, spinster, widow or widower. Lower life expectancy
  and high mortality rates during childbirth meant that it was not
  uncommon for our ancestors to marry more than once. Learning
  that an ancestor was widowed means you can search the death
  indexes to find out how a previous spouse died and when.

- **JOBS:** Once again, learning the profession of your ancestors
  means you can try and track down more information about
  them in their employment records as well as giving a flavour of
  their social status and standard of living.

- **ADDRESS:** The address of both bride and groom can come in
  very useful when cross-referencing or when you come to use

...h*Marylebone* in the County of *Middlesex*		
...dence at the Time of Marriage.	Father's Name and Surname.	Rank or Profession of Father.
...unt Paul *Deptford*.	*Rob.ᵗ Browning*	*Gent.ⁿ*
Marylebone	*Edw.ᵈ Barrett.*	*Gent.ⁿ*
...urch,	*by Licence*	by me,

your certificates in conjunction with the census.

- **FATHER'S NAMES:** This is the vital piece of information because it gives the researcher the information to take their search back a generation. If the father is dead, then 'deceased' will usually be written after their names.

- **FATHER'S PROFESSIONS:** This is another piece of the jigsaw, offering clues to social status and the opportunities for further research.

In the section across the bottom of the form you'll find another reference to the location of the wedding and whether the ceremony was performed by a marriage licence or banns. There's also a section signed by two witnesses to the wedding; often these were close friends but they might also be relatives of the bride and groom. This can be useful in identifying other siblings, and other branches of the tree to explore.

IC 618206

CERTIFIED COPY of an
Pursuant to the Births and

Registration District

1965. Death in the Sub-district of

No.	When and where died	Name and surname	Sex	Age	Occupation	Caus
10	Twenty-fourth January 1965. 28 Hyde Park Gate, Kensington	Winston Leonard Spencer Churchill	Male	90 Years	The Right Honourable. K.G. O.M, C.H, Statesman	(a) cerebra (b) cerebral c (1) congesta ate Mo

I, JOHN HEBBORN , Registrar of Births and Deaths for the Sub-district of
do hereby certify that this is a true copy of Entry No. 10 in the
Book is now legally in my custody.
WITNESS MY HAND this 26th day of January , 196

CAUTION.—Any person who (1) falsifies any of the particulars on this certificate, or
(2) uses a falsified certificate as true, knowing it to be false, is liable to prosecution.

Death Certificates

Death certificates are less valuable than their birth and marriage counterparts when it comes to genealogical information, but they are fascinating reading. They can also offer a clue about your ancestors' social standing, as well as the reason for their demise.

- **WHEN AND WHERE THEY DIED:** This will tell you where your ancestors died, whether it was at home or in hospital.
- **HOW OLD THEY WERE WHEN THEY DIED:** If you're producing a detailed family tree, then this is crucial information so you can enter details of your ancestors' lifespan. But it might also be the case that you've been unable to find

OF DEATH
Registration Act, 1953

7	8	9
Signature, description, and residence of informant	When registered	Signature of registrar
S.A.D. Montague Browne Present at the death 44 Eaton Place S.W.1	Twenty sixth January 1965	J. Hebborn Registrar.

, in the
of Deaths for the said Sub-district, and that such Register

J. Hebborn

Registrar of Births and Deaths.

A copy of Sir Winston Churchill's death certificate.

a birth and marriage certificate, in which case this becomes very useful. I couldn't find a marriage certificate for one of my great-grandfathers, Thomas Waddell, which prevented me from finding his birth certificate. I managed to find a death certificate, which told me he died aged 52, and allowed me to locate his birth certificate – and my previously stalled search was back on track.

- **OCCUPATION:** Again, these can be a useful pointer in finding employment records (as well as allowing you to track your ancestor's career from marriage to death).

- **CAUSE OF DEATH:** The most interesting piece of information on the form. Often these can be hard to decipher – for example, modern records have more specialized medical terms, which

will require further research. On older certificates, some causes
of death can be quite vague, even perplexing. 'Visitation by God'
meant someone who died inexplicably, perhaps in their sleep.
Its use was discouraged by the mid-nineteenth century but it
still shows up occasionally until around 1900. There are various
websites where you can find definitions of causes of death, but
www.archaicmedicalterms.com is especially good.

If the cause of death was an accident or, even more
exciting, a murder, then it's worth checking back copies of the
local newspaper to see if the death was reported in its news
pages, or whether an inquest was held and reported.

- **INFORMANT'S INFORMATION:** This gives the details of
  the person who registered the death. If it was a family member, it
  might give you another lead to follow.

Where to Find Them

In the past, at the late, lamented Family Records Centre in London
there were bound, searchable indexes of every birth, marriage and
death (BMD) certificate issued. These indexes could be searched to
find a reference which was then used to order the actual certificates
from the General Register Office (GRO). But these indexes are no
longer open to public inspection. In their place, several companies
and websites have created searchable online databases and the
majority of local libraries and record offices have the indexes on
microfiche. It is entirely up to you which method you choose.
Some websites charge a fee for using their indexes, but they also
offer a wealth of other information for that money. But it is worth
considering that, after you have found their reference number,
ordering the actual certificates can cost you a significant amount
of money too. At the time of writing, a copy of a birth, marriage

or death certificate from the GRO (www.gro.gov.uk) costs £9.25 including postage (the priority service, which means the document is sent to you within 24 hours, costs £23.40).

BMD certificates are essential to tracing your family tree. You will need to order as many as possible to be successful in your search and therefore it can be the most expensive part of your quest. It is worth deciding how much you're willing to spend before subscribing to any websites (see below) to ensure you have enough money left over to order the documents you need. But, whether you use an online database or the microfiche indexes at your local library or record office, the information you need to order the document remains the same. You need to have the reference number (the volume and page number), together with the name of the person you're searching for, the year of the event and the district in which it took place, to allow them to find your certificate quickly (the GRO will find you a certificate if you provide just the name, approximate date and district/area, but it will take much longer).

There are several sites that will allow you to search and find BMD records.

- **www.freebmd.org.uk** allows users to search more than 250 million records without charge. It has records from 1837 to 1983 but they have not yet transcribed all the records for the whole period.
- **www.ancestry.co.uk** is the most comprehensive genealogical 'one-stop shop' on the Internet. As well as BMD records, it has a vast range of databases of different records and documents from all around the world. Access to these records does not come free, however. Subscription at the time of writing was £12.95 a month or £107.95 a year.

- **www.findmypast.co.uk** also has a range of records as well as BMD indexes. It offers monthly and annual subscriptions of £9.95 and £99.95, respectively, although you can buy credits and 'pay as you go'.

Five BMD Tips

1. If you know the names of both ancestors who married, it's best to search for the one with the most unusual, or less common, surname.

2. Births and marriages were often registered shortly after the event, but deaths sometimes took several weeks to be entered and may show up in the index later than you are expecting.

3. Sometimes you might come across more than one possible match for your ancestor. The only way to solve that problem is to order all certificates and cross-reference the information on them with what you already know to find the correct one.

4. Sometimes you might only know certain dates. For example, you might know your grandfather was born in 1940. But you don't know when his parents (your great-grandparents) were married. In which case, work backwards initially, checking each year until you find a marriage certificate.

5. Be aware that the surname of the person you're searching for might be spelled in different ways.

Scotland

The Scots have their own registration process, which began later than England and Wales in 1855. If you have Scottish antecedents then the good news is you have an advantage because all their certificates offer more information than their English equivalents. For example, birth certificates carry all the information that English and Welsh ones do, with the added bonus of the date and place of the parents' marriage, which can save a lot of time finding the marriage certificate. When you do find the marriage certificate, you will discover that it contains the names of both parents of the bride and groom, including maiden name, rather than merely that of the father. Meanwhile, death certificates also give the names of both the deceased's parents.

The General Register Office of Scotland held the records and recently merged with the National Archives of Scotland to form the National Records of Scotland (NRS). The Statutory Registers index can be searched at www.scotlandspeople.gov.uk, as well as a range of other Scottish records.

Northern Ireland

All registration records from Northern Ireland since its creation in 1922 are held at the General Register Office of Northern Ireland in Belfast, as well as the original register for births and deaths in the region from 1864. Certificates cost £15 (£35 for a priority certificate) and can be ordered from www.nidirect.gov.uk.

Republic of Ireland

Civil registration of all births, marriages and deaths was introduced to Ireland in 1864 (although Protestant marriages were recorded from April 1845). The certificates provide the same information as their English and Welsh counterparts. There is a free online index at familysearch.org/search/collection/1408347, and a similar index for the same date range is available at findmypast.ie and www.ancestry.com. Certificates can also be ordered online at www.welfare.ie/pages/apply-for-certificates.aspx.

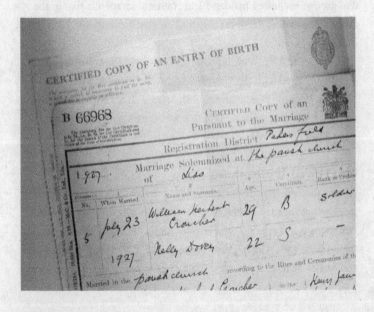

*Copies of a birth and a
marriage certificate.*

Starting from Scratch

Some people don't have living relatives who can supply information, or anyone else who can give them dates, names or a treasure trove of heirlooms and documents. But don't be disheartened. Here's a quick way to get started on your search:

1. Find or order your own birth certificate and note down your parents' names, including your mother's maiden name.
2. From the date of your birth, work out the approximate date of your parents' marriage and order their marriage certificate.
3. From the ages given on the certificate, work out the year of their birth and order each of your parents' birth certificates. (The certificate will also give you the names and occupations of your grandfathers.)
4. These birth certificates will give you the names of your grandparents. Pick either the maternal or paternal branch and return to step 2.

PATSY KENSIT

The actress Patsy Kensit began her journey with some trepidation. Her father, Jimmy Kensit, was a career criminal who had been involved with two notorious London family 'firms': the Krays and the Richardsons. For much of Patsy's childhood, Jimmy had been in and out of prison and her mother, Margaret, had done her best to shield Patsy and her brother from their father's gangland life. As a result, Patsy had little idea about her father's family, and now that both her parents were dead, it was too late to ask. So she set out to discover the truth, even though she was aware it might be unpalatable. 'So many secrets on so many levels,' she told the camera, but she said she was ready and willing to confront them.

HER BROTHER JAMES, whose godfather was Reggie Kray, retrieved a stack of photos and documents from his loft, which gave Patsy a starting point. From there she and James met criminologist Professor Dick Hobbs to learn more of her father's criminal career. He was first arrested in 1934 and had been in and out of jail for several years after. Eventually he found a role with the Richardson family carrying out 'long firm frauds': defrauding suppliers and customers by setting up apparently legitimate businesses.

* * *

But it was his childhood that intrigued Patsy. If she could learn more about it, perhaps she might understand how he become entangled in crime. All she knew of her paternal grandfather, also named James Kensit, was that he served in the First World War. At the National Archives she searched the medal roll index and discovered that he was a gunner in the Royal Field Artillery. However, after a 'civil conviction' he had been ordered to return his two war medals. The Calendar of Prisoners 1921, also held at the National Archives, revealed that James had convictions for nine criminal offences. Her father's role model had been a criminal, so it was unsurprising that he had fallen into the same line of work. Patsy was still determined to take her research back further but had grown fearful about what she might find. Would it be more criminality?

'No' was the answer, much to her relief. Her great-grandfather, yet another James, had been a 'walking stick finisher'. He lived in

Shoreditch at a time when 35 per cent of the East End's population lived below the poverty line. He would have been able to survive, but only just. It was a far cry from rural Beckenham, where he was born the illegitimate son of Sarah Kensit and James Dennis. The pair never married and the 1871 census reveals that Sarah and her son were living with her father, while James Dennis was still living with his dad, also James Dennis. James Dennis Senior turned out to be a pillar of the community, sexton of the local church, and enormously respected and loved. Patsy was moved to find someone like him in her family tree: a man who shared her religious faith.

Her next step was to see if she could take the Kensit line further back. She visited the London Metropolitan Archive to learn more about Thomas James Kensit, her great-great-grandfather, who had a flourishing walking-stick business in the 1850s and early 1860s. He was born in 1815, the son of Joseph Kensit, a goldbeater. Intrigued, Patsy visited the Worshipful Company of Goldsmiths where she learned that this highly skilled craft of beating gold until it was almost translucent had earned Joseph membership of the Goldsmiths' Company. Thomas inherited his father's membership and it was here that Patsy found out how her family's fortunes took a turn for the worse. Thomas had twice petitioned the company for financial support after the wooden walking stick business had collapsed. In the Goldsmiths' Company records, she read an account of how he had been forced to pawn his own coat for two shillings to feed his family.

Intriguingly, the records revealed that his wife was the daughter of Reverend James Mayne, curate of St Matthew's Church, Bethnal Green. The story was turning a full circle. Patsy had started her quest learning about criminality in east London, and was now in pursuit of an ancestor who had devoted much of his life to helping

London slum scenes at the turn of the 19th century. Off Louisa Place, Shoreditch, East London. Children skipping in the street.

the poor and needy of the same parish. James, her four times great-grandfather, was a remarkable man. He served 62,000 parishioners, performing all their baptisms, marriages and burials and keeping exhaustive records. If that wasn't enough, his pastoral duties included chaplaincy at a local lunatic asylum, founding a school and presiding over a charity that gave relief to the poor, whose subscribers included Prince Albert. Only 20 years after he set up this charity, his own daughter would be plunged into poverty.

James Mayne was a remarkable man. He was awarded the rare honour of a Lambeth degree by the Archbishop of Canterbury, and when his work in Bethnal Green was done, his earthly reward was to become vicar of a small church in Hanslow, Buckinghamshire. He is buried at the heart of the church beneath the altar.

It completed an incredible journey for Patsy: one that started with a discussion about criminal records and ended with her kneeling in a church over the memorial stone of an ancestor who had devoted his life to serving and helping others. Her dread at the start about what she might find had been replaced with great pride by the episode's conclusion. She felt more complete now that she knew the story of her father's family history. 'For the first time I feel as if I have two hands on my shoulders from my family's past,' she told the camera.

...age		

NAMES of each Person who abode therein the preceding Night.	AGE and SEX	
	Males	
...h Wilde		
... D°		
... D°		
...beth Morris		
...beth D°		
...iam D°	25	
...e Millard	25	
...rd Douville	10	
... Baker		

City or Borough of Sunderland			
nily	Condition	Age of	
		Males	Females
	Wid		31
		9	
			27
			11
		2	
			5
	Mar	48	
	Mar		23
			2
		2	
	Mar	25	
	Mar		36
			4
	Mar		10
			22
	u	55	
	u		24
	Mar		37
			5
			13
tal of Persons...		8	12

FIRST STEPS

Census Returns

FIRST STEPS
Census Returns

Towards the end of the eighteenth century, the state decided it needed to find a way to calculate how many people lived in the United Kingdom. The Government's main motivation was the prospect of invasion during the Napoleonic Wars and the need to know how many men were available to fight. The result was the first official census of 1801, which found that the population of the UK was nine million (the latest census in 2011 recorded 56.1 million). The census was not universally welcomed. In an echo of many of the debates we have today over civil liberties, there were those who believed such an act was the sign of an over-mighty executive, an infringement on human liberty and the right of man to live his life free from the beady eye of the state. That argument was lost and there has been a census every decade since (apart from 1941 when it was suspended for the Second World War).

* * *

The first four censuses of 1801, 1811, 1821 and 1831 are of minimal use to a family historian. They were, in the main, simple head counts, and those records that survive offer limited genealogical detail. There are some surviving records from the 1821 and 1831 censuses in certain regions which do offer more information, rather than merely how many people lived in a certain house, village or town. This was often done at the whim of the enumerator collecting the information, who knew the people he was 'counting' and decided to add some of their details.

A far more informative census, at least for genealogical purposes, started in 1841, when it was taken over by the General Register Office. From then on each census has listed the names of each person in every household in Britain. In 1851, the enumerators started to note the ages of those they recorded, making it an even more invaluable resource because it gives genealogists the opportunity to trace their ancestors even further back in time.

Here are some points to note about the census before we look at what information is available, where we can find it and how we can use it:

- The census is not released to the public until 100 years after it was taken. The most recently available census is from 1911 (which was released a few years ahead of schedule due to a ruling by the Information Commissioner). The next one available will be the 1921 census, which, at the time of writing, is not due for release until 2022.
- The census is a snapshot in time. It reveals who was in a property on the night it was taken, so it includes any staying guests.
- Some census returns have not survived the ravages of time or have gone missing, particularly some sections of the early censuses of 1841, 1851 and 1861. Most of Ireland's early census returns were destroyed by fire in 1922.

What the Census Tells Us

1841 Census

The 1841 census took place on 6 June 1841 and is generally referred to as the first 'modern census'. The information it provides is:

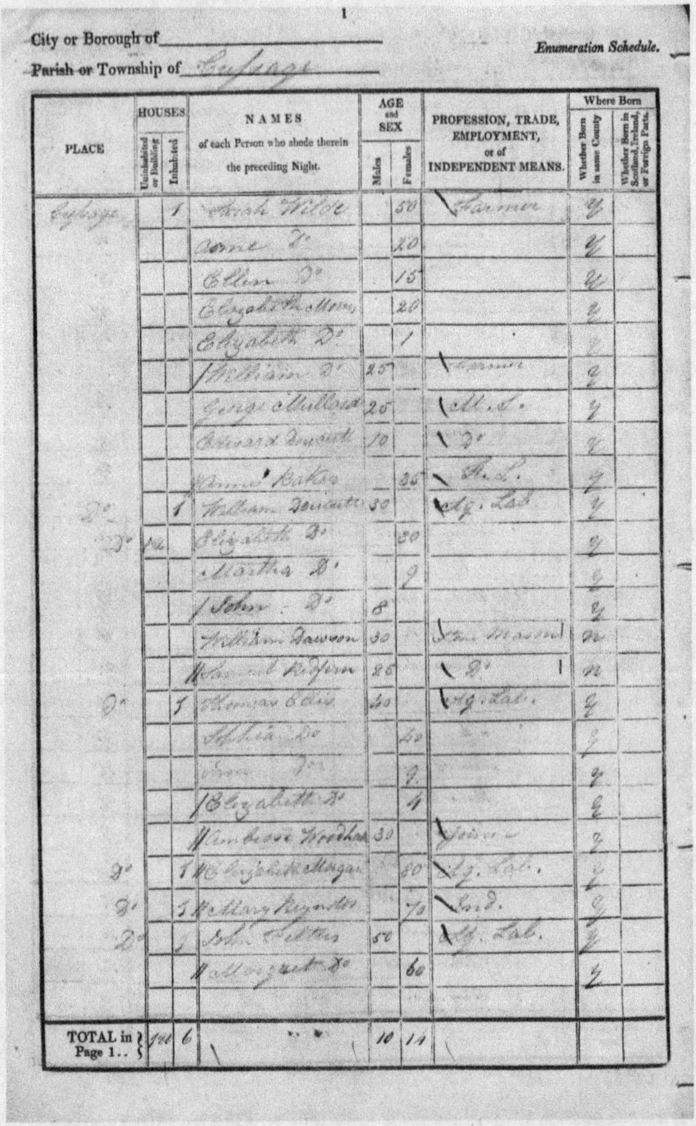

1

City or Borough of

Parish or Township of [illegible]

Enumeration Schedule.

PLACE	HOUSES: Uninhabited or Building	HOUSES: Inhabited	NAMES of each Person who abode therein the preceding Night.	AGE and SEX: Males	AGE and SEX: Females	PROFESSION, TRADE, EMPLOYMENT, or of INDEPENDENT MEANS.	Where Born: Whether Born in same County	Where Born: Whether Born in Scotland, Ireland, or Foreign Parts.
[illegible]		1	Sarah Wilde		50	Farmer	y	
			Anne Do		20		y	
			Ellen Do		15		y	
			Elizabeth Moore		20		y	
			Elizabeth Do		1		y	
			William Do	25		[illegible]	y	
			George Mulland	20		M. S.	y	
			Edward [illegible]	10		Do	y	
			Anne Baker		35	F. S.	y	
Do		1	William Dowcett	30		Ag. Lab.	y	
Do	1u		Elizabeth Do		30		y	
			Martha Do		9		y	
			John Do	8			y	
			William Dawson	30		Stone Mason	n	
			Samuel Redfern	25		Do	n	
Do		1	Thomas Ellis	40		Ag. Lab.	y	
			Sophia Do		40		y	
			[illegible] Do		7		y	
			Elizabeth Do		4		y	
			Ambrose Woodhead	30		Joiner	y	
Do		1	Elizabeth Morgan		80	Ag. Lab.	y	
Do		1	Mary Reynolds		70	Ind.	y	
Do		1	John [illegible]	50		Ag. Lab.	y	
			Margaret Do		60		y	
TOTAL in Page 1..	1u	6		10	14			

Census page for Sunderland East, Durham, 1851.

- **PLACE:** Your ancestor's address, although house numbers were not always recorded and in some rural areas the only information supplied is the name of the village.

- **NAME:** The people listed are those at that dwelling that evening. Unlike future censuses, no relation to the head of the household is given which can sometimes mean that making out who was who and what their relationships were is difficult.

- **AGE:** The exact age of those under 15 was recorded. But those over 15 had their ages rounded down to the nearest five, which means that someone who was listed as 30 might have been anywhere between 30 and 34. In some areas the actual age was recorded.

- **PROFESSION:** This section tells you what job your ancestor had, what rank he had if he was in the army, or if he or she was independently wealthy. Some occupations have been abbreviated. Some of the most common are:

  Ag. Lab. – Agricultural labourer

  Ap. – Apprentice

  Cl. – Clerk

  FS. – Female servant

  H.P. – Member of HM armed forces on half-pay

  Ind. – People with independent means

  J. – Journeyman

  M. – Manufacturer

  MS. – Male servant

- **PLACE OF BIRTH:** Unfortunately, this section only lets you know if your ancestor was born in the same county as they lived in. If they didn't, it doesn't tell you where they were born. If they were born in Scotland, Ireland or 'Foreign Parts', that would be noted with 'S', 'I' or 'FP', respectively.

I CERTIFY and declare that the Account of the Population of the District for which I am
by me, and that, to the best of my knowledge and belief, the same is correct.

Witness my hand this *Third* day of

I CERTIFY and declare that I have examined the Account of the Population contained in
on the day of *April* 1851, as

Witness my hand this day of

I CERTIFY and declare that I have examined the Account of the Population contained in
the *Twenty second* day of *April* 1851, and
same, and that no inaccuracies have been discovered therein which have not been duly corrected, as fa

Witness my hand this *fifth* day of

1851-1911 Censuses

These censuses record similar types of information, with only a few
differences (which are mentioned below) and for that reason can be
grouped together.

- **ADDRESS:** House numbers and street names were recorded, so
  it is easier to find out exactly where your ancestors lived.
- **MIDDLE NAME:** From 1851 it was more common to record

ained in this Book, has been truly and faithfully taken

1851.

Rogers _____ *Enumerator.*

is signed by the Enumerator, and was delivered to me
myself that it has been made as accurate as is possible.

1851.

_____ *Registrar.*

is signed by the Registrar, and was delivered to me
lly performed the duties required of him in regard to the
sible.

1851.

_____ *Superintendent Registrar.*

*Census page for Bickenhall,
Somerset, 1851.
Enumerator's signatures.*

middle names, or an initial at least, and increasingly common
thereafter. As before, every census was a snapshot of who was
there that night, so pray that your ancestor didn't decide to go
on a three-day drinking binge the night before!

- **RELATIONSHIP TO HEAD OF FAMILY:** A very helpful
  piece of genealogical data in drawing up a family tree. If your
  ancestors were wealthy, they might well have servants and they
  would be listed as such in the census. People were often judged

on their number of servants – the more you had, the richer you were – so this can offer an interesting glimpse of your ancestors' social standing (or their lack of it, if they were the servants!).

- **AGE:** These are no longer rounded down and so should be accurate, as long as the person was aware of his or her own age, which wasn't always the case. (Also give or take the odd white lie from those wishing to appear younger than they were...)

- **MARRIED:** Between 1851 and 1901, the census only recorded whether people were married or not. But in 1911 another piece of interesting information was added: how many years they had been married.

- **OCCUPATION:** Children at school were marked as 'scholar'. (Education wasn't compulsory until 1880, and then it was only between the ages of five and ten. In 1899 the leaving age was raised to 12.) The later censuses (1891 onwards) also recorded whether someone was an employer or an employee and the 1901 census identified those working at home.

- **BIRTHPLACE:** From 1851 onwards people were required to give their place of birth. This 'breakthrough', coupled with an accurate age, enables genealogists to find birth certificates from the census returns alone.

- **BLIND, DEAF OR DUMB:** This is self-explanatory, but in 1871 two extra categories were added: 'imbecile or idiot' and 'lunatic'.

Making Sense of the Census

The wealth of information available on a census return means it is possible to work out someone's story just from glancing at the return, and it also provides a starting point for hunting down certificates. Take a 1911 return, for example: you can discover the date someone was married, how soon after marriage they had children, how far apart their children were born, while the place of their and their children's birth will tell you how much or how little they had moved around. Their jobs give a fascinating glimpse into their lives, and by tracking them across various returns you can start forming a narrative of their life. Perhaps an ancestor started as a factory worker but gradually became a clerk and made the progression from blue to white collar. Also, by tracing your family back through census returns to 1841, if possible, you will gather the information and biographical detail you need to search for them before 1837 in the era of civil registration in parish registers.

It is also worth checking out your ancestor's neighbours. What sort of people lived in the adjoining houses? How many people lived there and what jobs did they do? It will give you a glimpse into the conditions they lived in. My father's family were coal miners and lived in coal-mining communities, sometimes 12 to a house. According to the 1881 census, my great-grandfather was working down the pit when he was 12 years old. Details like this can offer a real insight into the lives and hardships of your ancestors. You might also wish to see whether the houses your ancestors lived in are still standing. Visiting these places can be fascinating, and occasionally very moving. During series two of *Who Do You Think You Are?* Jeremy Paxman saw the tenement, then abandoned, where his single-mother ancestor was forced to raise her family in abject and unsanitary conditions. The experience was humbling and emotional for Jeremy. 'We just don't know we're born, do we?' he told the camera once he had recovered his composure.

The census can help you track your family and its ebb and flow through time. Through Scottish census records, the *Who Do You Think You Are?* team were able to build an extensive timeline of newsreader Fiona Bruce's family. These records showed the movements of the Bruce family around Hopeman, a seaside village in Scotland that Fiona believed to be the family's ancestral home, and allowed her to tour the village's streets and see the houses where her ancestors lived. They also enabled the researchers to trace several generations further back and find the first Bruce in Hopeman, George Bruce, Fiona's great-great-great-grandfather.

The census is vital for narrowing the search for birth, marriage and death certificates. For example, if you are looking for your great-grandparents' wedding certificate and you know your grandfather was born in 1909, you would ordinarily start searching back from that date. But if you were to examine the 1911 census and find out that he was the youngest of four children, the oldest of whom was ten in 1911, then you can start searching backwards from 1901, rather than 1909, and save yourself a great deal of work. Likewise, if you don't know when an ancestor died, rather than searching a wide range of dates for a death certificate, you can pinpoint the last census in which they appeared and begin your search from that date. Bill Oddie discovered in the 1901 census that his grandfather, Wilkinson Oddie, was listed as a widower. His oldest daughter Betsy was 12 and his youngest daughter Mary was seven. Armed with this information, Bill was able to track down a marriage certificate for Wilkinson and his wife, Cecilia, prior to 1889, and search for a death certificate for Cecilia between 1894 and 1901. He discovered that Cecilia died in 1897 during childbirth.

Census returns can also help you overcome any problems you might have locating civil registration records or tracking down that elusive ancestor. My great-grandfather Thomas Waddell and his wife, Maria, did not appear on the 1901 census, even though I had been told they were married by then. However, I hadn't been able to find a marriage certificate, even though I had birth and death certificates for them both. I had tried every single spelling of the surname Waddell I could think of with no luck. It felt like a dead end.

But I didn't give up. I went back to the 1881 census and there I found a Thomas Waddle who fitted all the details of the man I was looking for. He was living with a couple named William and Mary Wilson, as well as three children with the surname Waddle and three others named Wilson. They were of a similar age. His birth certificate had named his father as William Waddell and his mother Mary Waddell. What had happened?

I soon worked it out, with the aid of some death and marriage certificates. William Waddell had died in 1871, only a few months after Thomas was born. In 1874 Mary had married William Wilson, a widower, who also had children from his previous marriage. This was all very informative but it didn't tell me why Thomas had disappeared from the 1901 census. But the name on the 1881 census, Waddle (not Waddell as on his birth certificate) had given me a clue. I looked through the marriage indexes in the 1890s under Waddle and then under Weddle. At last I struck gold. A Thomas Weddle had married a Maria Harrison (which I knew to be my great-grandmother's maiden name) in 1895. I went to the 1901 census and there was Thomas Weddle, his wife and all the little Weddles. Not only had the 1881 census given me the clues to overcome the obstacle that had blocked my research, but in doing so I had learned a great deal about my great-grandfather's upbringing, the tragic loss of my great-great-grandfather and the existence of a previously unknown man, William Wilson, who raised Thomas as a son. The revelation in the 1881 census that my great-grandfather had a step-family also gave me a whole new chapter to explore in the future.

Where to Find Them

Most local and county record offices have microfilmed copies of each census from 1841 to 1901, but not 1911. So do the Family History Centres operated by The Church of Jesus Christ of Latter-Day Saints (these are worldwide – to find the nearest one visit https:// familysearch.org/locations/centerlocator). The National Archives in Kew (www.nationalarchives.gov.uk) has returns from 1841 to 1911 online, available free of charge.

There are a host of websites that offer searchable indexes and have scanned original returns, but most of them charge a fee. Here are some of the options to consider.

- **www.freecen.org.uk** is by no means complete, but it is free. Run by volunteers, its aim is to offer users the chance to search all nineteenth-century censuses (1841 to 1891) in one database. Coverage is growing all the time and it's worth checking out, particularly if you don't have the funds to pay for one of the commercial genealogy sites. The statistics page gives information about what percentage of each district has been transcribed for each census.
- **www.ancestry.co.uk** has complete national censuses from 1841 to 1911. It is possible to search each census by name. You can even use the search facility for free but it will cost to view the results. It also has transcriptions of Scottish census records between 1841 and 1901, as well as the 1901 and 1911 Irish censuses. Unlimited access to all records, not just census returns, is £12.95 a month or £107.95 a year.
- **www.findmypast.co.uk** has a full collection of census returns from 1841 to 1911 and was the first site to offer the 1911 census (in 2009). Like ancestry.co.uk, it is possible to search

for free but you will need to pay to see the results, either by subscription (£9.95 per month or £99.95 annually) or 'pay as you go'.

- **www.thegenealogist.co.uk** is another excellent commercial site which offers census returns from 1841 to 1911, as well as a vast range of other records. Different packages are available, ranging from £54.95 a year to £119.45.

Scotland

The Scottish census was taken in the same years as its English equivalent and it features much of the same information. The returns can be searched at www.scotlandspeople.gov.uk for a fee, while some regions are available to search for free at www.freecen.org.uk.

Ireland

Ireland did not start taking a census until 1821. As mentioned above, many of these records were destroyed during the Irish Civil War of 1922–3 and very few of the nineteenth-century records survive. The 1901 and 1911 censuses are available on the ancestry.co.uk website for a fee, but are also available at www.census.nationalarchives.ie for free. The good news is that they feature some additional information, too. The 1901 census reveals the religious denomination of your ancestors as well as the condition of their house! The 1911 census, like its English counterpart, reveals how long your ancestors had been married and the number of living children their marriage had borne. As Ireland was a united country at this point, these censuses also cover the counties that would later form Northern Ireland.

Where's My Ancestor?

Sometimes it can be tricky tracking our ancestors down on the census. Perhaps they're not where you expect them to be and occasionally you might not be able to locate them at all. Here are some common reasons why you can't find your ancestors and some tips on how to overcome them:

- **TRANSCRIPTION ERROR:** There are two mistakes which might result in your ancestor disappearing off the census. Firstly, an error made when the details were recorded. Secondly, errors can creep in when those records have been transcribed in recent years for searchable Internet databases. It can be difficult for modern eyes to decipher old-fashioned handwriting, and a small mistake can have far-reaching consequences. 'B's and 'D's can be confused, likewise 'a's and 'o's – there are several examples. If this is the case, then you'll need to consider other possible spellings and think laterally. If you have an idea of a street or area where your ancestor lived, it might be worth going to the original record rather than trusting someone else's data entry skills.

- **ANCESTRAL LIES:** It was your ancestors' responsibility on census night to supply the enumerator with accurate details. For a variety of reasons, they often didn't. People might have had to lie about their age to get a job and felt obliged to perpetuate the lie with an enumerator. Or someone might have been christened John but was known as Jack, and so the latter name was given. Then we have the desire to hide family secrets. Couples might adjust ages, or the date of marriage, so it appeared that a child was born in wedlock rather than out, or give an illegitimate child the family name to keep up appearances.

- **AWAY FROM HOME:** If your ancestor isn't listed at home, then perhaps he or she was in a workhouse, boarding at school or even in prison! They might have been soldiers and sailors who were stationed abroad, so check service records to see if they were away on service when the census was taken.

- **THEY AREN'T THERE:** In some censuses, up to five per cent of the population don't appear for a variety of reasons. They might have been homeless, for example. Or maybe they were like the author Agnes Strickland, who so loathed the idea that she spent census night of 1871 being driven around in a cab to avoid the enumerators.

SAMANTHA WOMACK

Actress and singer Samantha Womack described her own past as 'fractured'. Her parents separated when she was six and, according to Samantha, her father, the musician Noel Janus, was a man adrift in the world. He took his own life two years before her episode was filmed and she wanted to find someone in the family's past whom he might have been close to or identified with, as 'a gift from me to him'.

HER ANCESTRY was a blank canvas. A trip to her birthplace, Brighton, to visit her maternal grandmother, Dolly, yielded a number of names and leads. The one she chose to investigate first was her great-grandfather, Alexander Cunningham Ryan. Dolly remembered him as a 'sad man' who had been wounded in the war by a gas attack while serving with the Scots Guards.

* * *

Eager to know more, Samantha headed for Wellington Barracks, home of the Scots Guards. Alexander's service record revealed that, rather than being a victim of gas, he had been shot in the right lung from behind, probably by a German sniper. Samantha also discovered that he had been a musician and that, prior to joining the Scots Guards, he had served in the Highland Light Infantry (HLI) for 14 years. However, his service record with the HLI, which he joined as a 14-year-old boy soldier, only gave his length of service as eight years. Samantha was intrigued. Why had he lied to the Scots Guards?

She found that after leaving the HLI he re-enlisted with the Royal Garrison Artillery (RGA), a fact that he didn't mention to the Scots Guards. A journey to the RGA barracks in Plymouth produced an explanation – he had deserted and been convicted of a civil crime. Through prison registers and newspaper reports, Samantha found that Alexander had been in charge of the storeroom of musical instruments and had taken to pawning them, redeeming the loan when he earned enough money. But one day there was a check of the instruments and a silver-plated cornet was revealed to be missing. Alexander was sentenced to a month's imprisonment. In his absence he was given a dishonourable discharge from the army, which would have hung around his neck like a millstone. If he tried to re-enlist in the army he faced a two-year prison sentence. He managed to re-enter military life at the outbreak of the First World War by omitting any mention of his crime, but his military career was ended by a sniper's bullet. Samantha believed that her late father would have loved to have known about him and to have discovered that they shared a talent for and love of music.

Her attention now turned to Alexander's wife, Beatrice Garraud. All Samantha knew was her name, and that of her mother, Jessie Ryder. Given that she had so little information she turned to the venerable Society of Genealogists for help. Finding Beatrice and Jessie required some nifty lateral thinking but eventually Samantha found the marriage certificate of Jessie to Pierre Garraud in August 1892. There was more than a whiff of the shotgun about the wedding, as four months later their first child, Anthony, was born, followed two years later by Berthe, who would become Beatrice.

From there it grew more intriguing still. A death certificate for Anthony revealed that he had died, aged six, from burns after his nightdress caught fire. He was in an orphanage. Newspaper reports of the inquest said his clothing had caught fire after coming into contact with a lit gas stove. They also reported that his father was dead and that his mother was in the USA 'on the stage'. This conjured up a host of questions for Samantha. What was she doing in America? Why was her son in an orphanage? And where was Berthe/Beatrice?

*Samantha with her father,
the musician Noel Janus.*

*Samantha as
a young child.*

The 1901 census answered that last question. When she was nearly three in 1897, Beatrice was admitted to Nazareth House in Hammersmith, a charitable institution that cared for the elderly, infirm and children of the destitute. She remained there until she was eight, when she was taken in by her grandparents, who presumably could not afford to take in both her and her brother before his death.

Though she had now found Beatrice, it still begged many questions about Jessie. By searching passenger lists Samantha learned that she had travelled to and from New York in 1891 before her marriage. To find out if she was there after her children had been born, Samantha travelled to the Big Apple, where she was told that Jessie had been living in Jersey City in 1899. Astonishingly, she'd had another child, Annie Gertrude, and she was now Jessie Finkle. Newspaper cuttings from a few years later revealed she was a comedian and toured with her infant daughter, who also appeared on stage.

'I feel nothing but contempt for this woman,' Samantha told the camera, shocked that she'd had another child so shortly after her son had been killed and was cavorting on stage in America while her daughter languished in an orphanage back in England. Did she ever send for Beatrice? Samantha checked the 1910 census at Jersey City Library. Beatrice was there, along with Gertrude and another child, Harry Junior. In 1907, when Beatrice was ten, her mother and her new family had returned to England to collect Beatrice and bring her to America to live with them.

The knowledge that Jessie had eventually done the right thing offered Samantha some comfort. Indeed, the whole experience of tracing her unknown roots had given her a sense of peace. She realized there was a family she belonged to, many of whom, like herself and her father, had been performers, which gave her a sense of pride. 'It's been truly, truly healing,' she said. 'I will never have to ask those questions again: "Who are we? Where are we from?" Because now I know.'

BARTON UPON IRW[...]

in the County [...]

5	6
Name, surname and maiden surname of mother	Occupation of father
Kate Clarke formerly Kennedy	*Bankers Clerk*

a Register of Births in the District a[...]

he said Office, the 12th

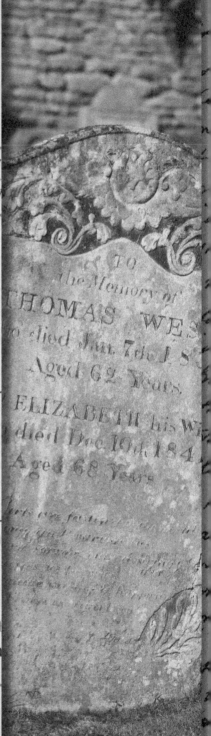

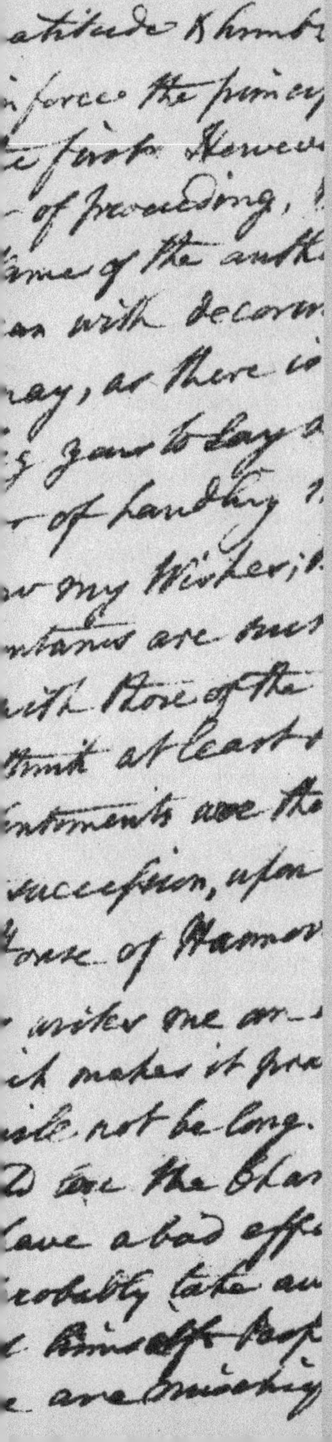
atitude & humb
n force the princ
e first. Howeve
of proceeding,
me of the autho
an with decorum
ay, as there is
g your to lay
r of handling
w my Wishes
ntances are
with those of the
think at least
ntiments are the
succession, upon
ouse of Hanov
writer one
ch makes it pro
ill not be long.
D see the
ave a bad effe
robably take
e are

NEXT STEPS

NEXT STEPS

By using civil registration documents in combination with census returns, aided by a good dose of luck, it should be possible for you to take your research back to the mid-nineteenth century. The trick is to use birth and wedding certificates in concert to take you beyond the 1911 barrier, where you can pick up the census, use it to narrow and focus your search and continue to journey back through the years. But it all comes to a grinding halt when you hit 1837 (for civil registration) and 1841 (for the census) and reach the period before the state began recording the lives of its citizens.

***

What happens next is entirely your decision. For some people, it's enough to know as much as they can about the lives of their recent ancestors rather than those in the distant past. I'm one of them. My focus was how my paternal family became involved in coal mining, which was explained in the civil registration era. Beyond that, there are leads back to rural Scotland and Ireland. One day I might take up those leads and learn more about my early ancestry, but for now my aim is to continue digging out as much information as I can about recent generations, rather than searching for those who lived 200 years ago or more. If that's what you want to do, then the next few chapters will suggest ways you can flesh out the bones of your family tree, and learn more about the people they were, the lives they led and the times in which they lived.

But many people understandably want to take their research as far back as possible and to trace their family tree way into the mists of early modern history. Or they have discovered an interesting ancestor in the early days of the civil registration era and want to find out more about them and their family, which means working with records pre-1837, collected on a local level rather than by the state. This section deals with how to do that.

Archive Dos and Don'ts

At some stage in your ancestral quest you'll have to visit archives or record offices. These can sometimes be intimidating places, especially for those new to research, but there's no reason to worry. Here are some tips to help you get the most out of your visit:

Do

- **PREPARE FOR YOUR VISIT:** Make sure you visit the archive's website or call in advance to check things like opening times, access to information, whether you need to book a time to visit and what documentation you might need to register, if required. By all means contact the archive staff in advance and ask if they have the information you're looking for – you might save yourself much expense and time!
- **ASK STAFF:** Most staff are well trained, friendly and know exactly what they're doing and what information their archive holds. Never be afraid of asking them for help, whether that's about where to find information, how to feed microfilm into a reader or where the nearest pencil sharpener is!

- **BE REALISTIC:** This applies not only to what and how much information you will find, but also how much time it might take to search the archive. Sometimes you might come across new leads or discoveries that open up different avenues of investigation, so make sure you set aside enough time to do all the research that you need to do. A few hours might not be enough!

Don't

- **IGNORE ARCHIVE RULES:** The material you might be handling is often old and worn, sometimes unique and priceless. Every archive has rules about how to handle its material. Make sure you're well acquainted with them before you start your research, to avoid being thrown out! For example, most archives only allow people to use pencils and not biros. Drinking and eating are usually prohibited.

- **ANNOY YOUR FELLOW RESEARCHERS:** Most archives insist on silence so people can get on with their work without interruption or nuisance. Satisfying as it might be, punching the air and shouting for joy when you track down that elusive ancestor is frowned upon in the research community. Make sure your mobile phone is switched off (or on silent if you're in an archive that allows you to use it to photograph material) and if you take a friend or relative, as people often do, make sure your conversations are brief and quiet.

- **ASSUME:** This applies across the board. If you can't
find information, don't assume it's not in the archive.
Or, if someone is taking photos of documents, don't
assume you can, too. Whenever you're in doubt, ask a
member of staff. They are there to help.

Parish Records

The good news is that there are birth, marriage and burial records
which pre-date the era of civil registration. The bad news is that
many have been lost or damaged. The other piece of bad news is that
there are no centralized indexes of parish registers, as with birth,
marriage and death certificates and the census, although there are
several websites that have collected vast amounts of local data and
made it available online.

Historically speaking, a parish was a small administrative
district, which had its own church and a local priest or pastor. Their
existence in the United Kingdom dates back more than 1,500 years.
Since the Reformation, when England broke away from the Catholic
Church under Henry VIII's rule in the sixteenth century, the vast
majority of parishes have belonged to the Church of England.
The records of the small minority of Catholic churches and other
religious denominations that were allowed to worship are known as
'nonconformist records'.

In 1538, a new law required every Church of England priest to
record all baptisms, marriages and burials in his parish. 'Great,'
you might think, 'I can trace my family back to the mid-sixteenth

ST. PAUL'S PARISH, NORWICH.

Amelia Daughter of Thomas Elizabeth Clithnow th Dn

was Born *15th June 1829* and Baptized *21st June 1829*.
as appears by the Register of the aforesaid Parish.

York Curk Chnton
21st July 1845

Birth register entry
from St. Paul's Parish,
Norwich, 1829.

century.' Not unless you're very fortunate. Luck plays a major part in tracing early ancestry. The favoured few might be able to trace their ancestral trail back to the seventeenth century, and even the sixteenth in some remarkable cases. The less blessed will be lucky to go back into the eighteenth century. Many early records were poorly kept and have not survived, while some of those which have are no longer legible. We are also at the mercy of the individual priest or pastor or the person he appointed as his clerk. Each had their own method and system. Some had separate registers for baptisms, marriages and burials, while others collected them on the same register. As the years progressed, the process became more standardized and it is more likely that you will find out something about your ancestors. Just hope the man who recorded the significant events of your ancestor's life was an assiduous, thorough fellow rather than a dilettante who left all his record-keeping until the night before his annual register was due.

It is worth noting that, theoretically speaking, parish records are still kept to this day. If you have been unable to track down an ancestor's civil birth, marriage or death records, then it's worth checking their local parish register, in particular during the early days of civil registration when it was widely disliked and people were more likely to entrust record-keeping to their church. It can also be useful to find a parish record to cross-reference with a civil registration one if you're unsure about the information you find in the latter.

What Can I Learn?

Baptisms

Baptism records often give only the date of baptism and not the date of birth. They can vary in detail depending on the source, but early records (sixteenth and seventeenth century, for example) offer very basic information: in most cases, the name of the child and the father's name only. But even information this sparse can be crucial. During her episode, the fashion model Jodie Kidd was able to track down a baptism record for one of her ancestors from 1631, which proved the family line had started in Yorkshire, before the family left England for New England.

The Rose Act 1813 issued all parishes with pre-printed books in which to record their baptisms, marriages and burials, and more information was noted after that date, such as when the baptism took place, the name of both parents, where they lived, a profession or trade, and the name of the person conducting the ceremony.

Marriages

Like with most parish records, what information you'll discover about your ancestor's marriage is pot luck. You should be able to find the names of both bride and groom and the date of their marriage. There is also a chance you might come across the name of the bride's father and, if you're really lucky, an occupation for the groom. Jodie Kidd was fortunate; she was able to find records of her ancestor's marriage from September 1624. Like many records of the time, they were written in Latin. Don't despair if that's the case and you're lacking a grounding in the classics, because there's rarely more than a sentence or two and most archives have Latin dictionaries which can help you translate and understand the text.

Burials on Ireland Island for the year 1842 69
Continued.

Date	Name	Occupation	By Whom Interred
3rd April	William McGurk	Convict, Dromedary	Robert Mantach
6th April	Thomas Vaughan	Convict, Dromedary	Robert Mantach
7th April	Jane Charlotte Beresford	wife of B.S. Beresford Captn. Royal Artillery	Robert Mantach
12th April	Mary Sanders	wife of P. Sanders Stone Mason	Robert Mantach
17th April	William Paton	son of Serjeant Paton R. Sappers & Miners	Robert Mantach
24th April	Peter Tucker	Hospital Nurse, man of Colour from Southampton &c.	Robert Mantach
25th April	Samuel Welford	Convict, Dromedary	Robert Mantach
29th April	Charlotte Hurd	a Child — R.S.M.	Robert Mantach
4th May	William Dixon	Convict, Coromandel	Robert Mantach
10th May	John Holmes	Convict, Dromedary	Robert Mantach
15th May	William Shuley	Convict, Dromedary	Robert Mantach
19th May	John Downton	Seaman H.M.S. Warspite Marine.	Robert Mantach
26th May	John King	Convict, Dromedary	Robt. Mantach

Robert Mantach
Off: Clergyman.

Record of baptisms and burials on Ireland Island, Bermuda, 1842.

The records might also tell you whether your ancestors were married by 'banns' or licence. Banns of marriage were posted in the parish church before the wedding for the public to see, thus allowing them to raise any concerns or reasons why the couple in question should not be married (if one party was already married, for example, or if the parties were too closely related...). If your ancestors chose to marry by licence, it probably meant they were slightly better off than their fellow parishioners because it was comparatively expensive. Few licences still exist but 'allegations' do. These were a vowed intention to marry and bore the names of the engaged couple, their ages, the parish where they lived, the groom's occupation and the name of their parents: all priceless information.

Burials

We have been compelled to bury the dead for thousands of years. Thankfully, for the past few hundred years we have also been compelled to keep records of those burials. Unfortunately, some early parish registers contain little useful genealogical information, just the name of the deceased and little else, not even an age. But they can still be valuable. On his journey into his ancestry Kevin Whately used burial records to find the grave of his four-times great-grandmother Mary Thompson, who died in 1776. The vicar of the church in whose graveyard she was buried gave him a copy of the inscription written on her tomb, which gave Kevin a wealth of genealogical information, including where she and her husband lived and the name of her father.

From the mid-eighteenth century onwards, it became common to record age and details such as occupation, next of kin or address. But often more information was recorded on the dearly departed's tombstone than in the registers.

Gravespotting

If you manage to track down your ancestors' burial place, why not pay their final resting place a visit? Municipal cemetery records can often be found at your local record office, which can tell you the location of the grave, often with a handy map. Then it's just a matter of hoping that time and mother nature have not taken too much of a toll on your ancestor's tombstone, because the inscriptions can give valuable clues and information, such as a job, names of children or next of kin, even a message or quote from scripture or literature. It can be a truly humbling experience, especially if your graveyard visit is the culmination of many months or years of searching for information about your ancestor.

If you don't know where your ancestors might be buried, www.deceasedonline.com is a wonderful new resource that allows you to search its database of statutory burial and cremation registers for the UK and Republic of Ireland.

Nonconformist Records

If your ancestors weren't Anglicans, don't panic. They were in a minority but by no means a small one – the 1851 census revealed that 25 per cent of the country was nonconformist. Many of these groups' registers are housed at the National Archives in Kew, and a number of them have been made available online. Various Protestant dissenting groups, such as the Quakers and Moravians, were diligent record-keepers. After the Reformation, Catholicism was effectively outlawed and those who followed the faith were often persecuted for their beliefs. For this reason, few records survive from the sixteenth to eighteenth centuries. If you discover Catholic ancestors it is worth checking at the National Archives for details of any fines or penalties imposed on them for practising Catholicism (they were called recusants).

Where to Find Them

Most collections of parish records are deposited at the local or county record archive or office for that district. If you're not sure where that might be, contact your local council and it should be able to point you in the right direction. The originals are too delicate or degraded to be used by the public, so you'll be searching copies on microfilm or microfiche. This can be fiddly, so it's always best to have a member of staff show you how to use them before you end up with reels and reels of film on the floor! It's also worth seeking out your local family history society to see what records they might have, while the Family History Centres run by The Church of Jesus Christ of Latter-Day Saints can order copies of parish registers on request.

A number of websites offer access to parish registers. As with all online databases, there is no guarantee of accuracy and it is always worth trying to locate the original source of the material before accepting the information as truth. But the following are some that offer the most complete collections:

• **www.familysearch.org** is compiled by The Church of Jesus Christ of Latter-Day Saints, but the database is also available to all researchers for free. The Church has sent people across the globe to gather a mass of genealogical material to allow its members the chance to research their family tree in order to baptize their ancestors into the religion. Their collection covers every continent and features three billion names. Among those are a vast range of baptisms, as well as some marriage and burial records from England, Wales, Scotland and Ireland. The site is easy to use, all of which makes it a crucial tool for genealogists.

- **www.freereg.org.uk** is a companion site to the previously mentioned FreeBMD and FreeCen websites. Like those sites, and as its name suggests, it's completely free to use. At the time of writing the database contained nearly 4.5 million marriages, 13.5 million baptisms and more than nine million burials.

- **www.thegenealogist.co.uk** offers a vast collection of genealogical material, including a wide range of parish and nonconformist records, which are constantly being added to. There are a wide range of subscription offers available.

- **www.findmypast.co.uk** has a growing range of parish records from 1538–2005, many of them transcribed and indexed by family history societies. New records are added regularly.

Scotland and Ireland

Most surviving Scottish parish registers date back to the late seventeenth or eighteenth century, when the Presbyterian Church became the country's established church. Though they don't go back as far, the records themselves are often more detailed than their English counterparts. For example, baptisms often record the mother's maiden name. But, like in England, the amount of information you might find is variable. Many registers are available to search and view at www.scotlandspeople.gov.uk.

Sadly, some Irish parish registers endured the same fate as the country's census records: destruction by fire during the Irish

Civil War. Those records that did survive are held at the National Archives of Ireland in Dublin, the National Library of Ireland and the Representative Church Body Library, while many parish churches have kept their original records. There are also websites that offer access to millions of Irish parish records including www. irishgenealogy.ie and wwww.rootsirelend.ie.

Reading Old Handwriting

Parish registers date back hundreds of years, to a time before standardized spelling. Our modern eyes, accustomed as they are to the printed word, may struggle to decipher the ornate, elegant text woven by the hands of our forebears. All of this can make old documents difficult to read. Often it's a case of experience – the more old texts you read, the easier you find it to understand them. But if you find a particularly impenetrable piece of text then don't be afraid to ask a member of staff at an archive to help you make sense of it. The National Archives also provides a useful online tutorial in palaeography (the study of old handwriting), focusing on documents written in English between 1500 and 1800, which can be found at www.nationalarchives.gov.uk/palaeography.

O say can you see ~~through~~ by the dawn's early light,
What so proudly we hail'd at the twilight's last gleaming,
Whose broad stripes & bright stars through the perilous fight,
O'er the ramparts we watch'd, were so gallantly streaming?
And the rocket's red glare, the bomb bursting in air,
Gave proof through the night that our flag was still there,
O say does that star spangled banner yet wave
O'er the land of the free & the home of the brave?

On the shore dimly seen through the mists of the deep,
Where the foe's haughty host in dread silence reposes,
What is that which the breeze, o'er the towering steep,
As it fitfully blows, half conceals, half discloses?
Now it catches the gleam of the morning's first beam,
In full glory reflected now shines in the stream,
'Tis the star-spangled banner — O long may it wave
O'er the land of the free & the home of the brave!

And where is that band who so vauntingly swore,
That the havoc of war & the battle's confusion
A home & a Country should leave us no more?
~~Their blood~~
Their blood has wash'd out their foul footsteps' pollution.
No refuge could save the hireling & slave
From the terror of flight or the gloom of the grave,
And the star-spangled banner in triumph doth wave
O'er the land of the free & the home of the brave.

O thus be it ever when freemen shall stand
Between their lov'd home & the war's desolation!
Blest with vict'ry & peace may the heav'n rescued land
Praise the power that hath made & preserv'd us a nation!
Then conquer we must, when our cause it is just,
And this be our motto — "In God is our trust,"
And the star-spangled banner in triumph shall wave
O'er the land of the free & the home of the brave.

'Star Spangled Banner', 1814. Francis Scott Key's hand-written
manuscript of 'The Star Spangled Banner', which he wrote
at the Fountain Inn, Baltimore, after witnessing the British
bombardment of Fort McHenry on September 13-14, 1814.

Where There's a Will

It's a well-worn myth that people become interested in family history because they hope to find an unclaimed legacy that will make them rich. But occasionally people do find something surprising in the last testaments of their ancestors. Take broadcaster Jeremy Clarkson, for example. He discovered that when one of his maternal ancestors died he left his son £1 million in his will. Jeremy, hitherto equivocal about his family history, was more interested. 'What happened to the cash?' he wondered, unsurprisingly. As it turned out, it wasn't laying unclaimed but was frittered away by Caleb's descendants, much to Jeremy's disappointment. The actor Kevin Whately also discovered a wealthy ancestor. By the time of his death, his great-grandfather Frederick Phillips had built up a business which would have been worth £2 million in today's money. Sadly, the business dwindled and died after his demise.

Whether our ancestors were rich, comfortably off or poor, wills are an excellent resource for family historians. They are a treasure trove of genealogical information. You can find names of extended family members, work out the relationship between people and discover previously unknown occupations and addresses. By noting who was included in wills and who was left out, you can build up a picture of your family's dynamics and investigate family feuds – some wills go into great detail to explain why certain people are excluded! It's also possible to get a glimpse of the personality of the people who wrote the wills – what they valued, who they valued, and any charities or organisations they might have bequeathed money to. There might also be an inventory of their possessions, which offers another fascinating insight into their lives.

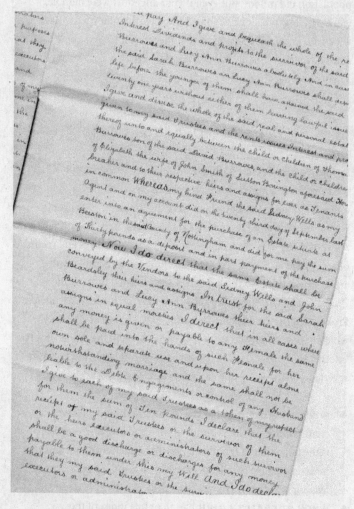

Copy of the Will of Mrs
Harvey of Nottingham,
17 November 1846.

Of course, not everyone made a will. Only one in ten of the population did in 1901. But even if your ancestors were humble, working-class folk, don't be fooled into believing they won't have left a will. People of all classes wrote them, even it was simply to hand down their best milking cow or favourite flat cap. It's always worth checking.

Where to Find Them

People have made wills for hundreds of years. Prior to 1858 wills were proved at a number of ecclesiastical courts of the Church of England, the highest of which were the Prerogative Court of Canterbury and the Prerogative Court of York. This means that many of those wills are scattered across various archives and record offices. Since 1858, wills have been administered centrally and are therefore easier to track down. They are listed in the National Probate Calendar, which is available in most archives. The Principle Probate Registry in Holborn, London, holds copies of all wills which have been proved since 1858 and is open to the public. But the Internet is also an excellent resource for will-hunting and there are several websites where one can start searching for that elusive legacy.

- **www.origins.net** has the National Will Index, which contains more than four million wills and probate records. It is the largest online source of pre-1858 material and includes material that isn't available anywhere else online. Subscription fees apply.
- **www.ancestry.co.uk** has an online index of the Prerogative Court of Canterbury, which includes the wills of William Shakespeare, Jane Austen, William Wordsworth and Oliver Cromwell. It is also the only site to feature the National

Probate Calendar., which is searchable by name, between 1858 and 1966. It tells you when and where your ancestor died and the size of any estate. This can then be used to order the copies of the will for the extra information it provides. A subscription is necessary to view the image results of your search.

- **www.scotlandspeople.gov.uk** boasts a wills and testaments index which contains over 611,000 index entries dating from 1513 to 1925. Each index entry lists the surname, forename, title, occupation and place of residence (where applicable) of the deceased, the court in which the testament was recorded, as well as the date. The site also has images of wills and testaments for that period.

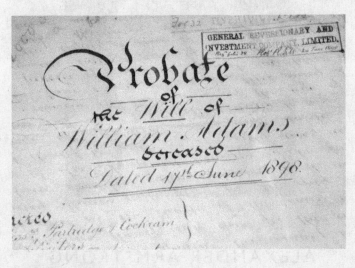

Handwritten Probate of the Will of William Adams from 1898. Written on vellum.

ALEXANDER ARMSTRONG

In one episode of his comedy show *Armstrong and Miller*, Alexander Armstrong performed a spoof sketch of *Who Do You Think You Are?* in which he imagined he was linked to nobility, but ended up being related to a string of prostitutes. When he came to appear on the show itself, he was hoping to find dark secrets and noble bloodlines and not just a line of 'chinless wonders'. He wasn't to be disappointed.

HIS STORY BEGAN at his family home in Northumberland. His father's line has already been well documented, but he knew less about his mother's family, the McCauslands, other than that they owned a stately home in Northern Ireland, where she grew up and he visited as a child. His aim was to discover from where the family 'stature' and wealth originated.

***

He managed to trace his maternal line back to Mary Boughton, his six-times great-grandmother, who in 1761 was made one of Queen Charlotte's six bedchamber-women. She had two sons, Sir Edward and Sir Charles. Edward, the eldest, was a ne'er-do-well who ended up borrowing an enormous amount from his more responsible younger brother. Alexander was shown a letter in which Edward celebrated the 'wonderful news' about the death of their cousin, Theodosius, who was a baron. This meant that Edward would inherit the baronetcy and the family's estate, thus ending his financial woes.

However, the circumstances of Theodosius' death proved to be murky. His body was exhumed and physicians ruled that he had been poisoned. Alexander did briefly wonder if Edward had been involved, given his delight at his cousin's demise. But it emerged that the suspected murderer was Theodosius' brother-in-law, Captain John Donellan. From the trial record in 1780, Alexander learned that the prosecution claimed the captain had poisoned his brother-in-law with laurel water to seize his inheritance. In his defence, the captain

Alexander as a boy (centre) with brother Dominic (far left), mother Emma (left), father Henry (right) and sister Alice (far right).

Alexander as a child.

said that Theodosius had contracted venereal disease after spending so much time with prostitutes at boarding school. His syphilis, as was the custom, had been treated with mercury, which has many toxic side-effects. It seems clear that this adequately explained Theodosius' death, but nevertheless Donellan was found guilty and hanged.

Alexander was worried. Both Theodosius and Edward seemed prime examples of the chinless, dissolute wonders he was loathe to find. But Sir Charles, a successful MP, seemed to be made of far sterner stuff. When Alexander learned that Edward left the family estate to his illegitimate daughters in his will, rather than Charles as would have been the custom, he was even more aghast. Charles was intent on a political career in the House of Lords and the wealth created by the estate would qualify him for ennoblement. But his hopes had been dashed by his brother's ingratitude. Charles had leant Edward a fortune over the years and in return his dreams had been thwarted.

From Mary Boughton, Alexander traced his bloodline back three more generations to Henry Somerset, the 1st Duke of Beaufort. Here, Alexander proclaimed, was real aristocracy rather than mere landed gentry. Henry, his ten-times great-grandfather, was a close friend of Charles I. During the English Civil War, he had bankrolled the Royalist war effort to the tune of £70 million by today's money. Not only that, he had raised his own army of 2,000 men to fight for the cause. Unfortunately, he chose to travel to Oxford to meet the King one day and left his regiment behind, only for parliamentarian forces to steal upon them and capture almost every single man without a shot being fired.

Charles still trusted Henry so much that he asked him to go on a top-secret mission to Ireland to raise troops from the Catholic Confederates. This was highly controversial – only three years before, the Catholics had fought a bloody rebellion against their British rulers and now here they were asking the same men to fight on their side. News of the mission leaked, there was a brouhaha, and the King had no option but to deny all knowledge of the mission and impeach his friend for high treason. But he did use his influence to save Henry from being executed and he served the remainder of the war in prison.

The war over, Henry went back to his first love – science. Alexander was delighted to find out his ancestor was a 'crackpot' inventor who wrote about experiments such as trying to get a man to fly. His pride and joy was a 'water commanding' engine which he wanted to be buried alongside him. Alexander travelled to the Science Museum in London to learn more about this contraption. He discovered that rather than being a crackpot, Henry was ahead of his time. His water machine was one of the earliest steam machines, built 40 years before the pioneers of steam power harnessed it to such transformative effect.

Alexander saw a diagram of the machine but, even more deliciously, he was told that Henry was so revered in engineering circles by the mid-nineteenth century, that a macabre plan was hatched to dig into his grave and retrieve his wondrous machine. He was shown a gruesome account of the recovery team's exploration of the tomb – but the model wasn't found. However, for a group of enthusiasts to be rooting in his grave after 200 years, for a contraption which was ignored in his lifetime, was a real honour, according to Alexander. 'What a fantastic man,' he said of Henry.

All that remained was to trace Alexander's bloodline as far back as possible. At the College of Arms he learned that William the Conqueror was his twenty-seven-times great-grandfather. Alexander ended his journey feeling profoundly lucky that he came from such a richly chronicled lineage. 'From a personal, and slightly smug point of view, there's something absolutely thrilling about these discoveries,' he said.

SECRETS
AND
SCANDALS

SECRETS AND SCANDALS

For many of us, one of the great joys of family history is finding the secret that no one in the family knew about. I stumbled across one within ten minutes of starting to investigate my family tree. No one had done the research before, so it was like treading virgin snow. I asked my father when my grandparents, both dead, had married. '1936,' he said. 'Four years before I was born.' I checked the marriage indexes for that year and found nothing. Likewise, 1937, 1938 and 1939. For the sake of completeness I checked 1940. There they were. They had married four *months* before my father was born, which was a bit of a story given my grandmother was a devout Catholic (although obviously not *that* devout).

* * *

Stories like mine pepper many people's research and crop up time and again in the show. Many of us embrace them – they prove our ancestors are human, with flaws and foibles just like us, and not remote, distant figures in sepia-tinted photographs or printed names on census returns. History isn't just about heroes – it's about villains, too. A rogue ancestor offers a fun line of investigation, as we try and delve into their crimes and misdemeanours. But always be aware that there are members of your family who might be shocked to hear of such events, so handle the information you come across sensitively and don't expect everyone to embrace the truth as readily as you!

Here are some of the most common 'scandalous' themes and subjects you might encounter in your research, and how to take your research further if you're lucky enough to encounter a 'black sheep' in your family.

Adoption

In her episode, Lesley Sharp, the actor, revealed that she was raised by adopted parents and wanted to know more about the ancestry of her birth family. Even if we weren't adopted like Lesley, many of us will find cases of adoption in our family tree, and research is not straightforward. But here's a quick guide to finding out more.

Before 1927

There was no legal framework for adoption before this time, so there is no guarantee of surviving records. Those records that do exist were kept by the charity or orphanage that organized the adoption. Dr Barnardo's organization was heavily involved in children's care and it is worth contacting if you believe it may have taken in your ancestor.

After 1927

The Adoption of Children Act of 1926 made adoption a legal process from January 1927. Adoptions were entered into an Adopted Children Register. The index is available to the public in certain places and can be searched at Westminster City Archives from 1927-2011 on microfiche, and at the British library and some regional libraries. If you wish to search it you will need the child's adoptive name and date of birth in order to find a birth certificate. For anyone wishing to locate their birth parents, a good first port of call is the Adoption, Search and Reunion website www.adoptionsearchreunion.org.uk.

Illegitimacy

In the past, illegitimate children were a shameful secret, particularly at the height of the prudish Victorian era. But that doesn't mean they weren't common. They were, and a number of us will encounter this during our research, although it's not something our ancestors shouted about. The telltale signs include a blank on a birth certificate where a father's name should be, or a large gap between the birth dates of the last two children on a census return, particularly if the parents are almost beyond child-bearing age but there is an unmarried eldest or older daughter of child-bearing age. There's a chance the child might be theirs, but listed as belonging to its grandparents to avoid calumny.

Amanda Redman, the actor famous for her role in detective drama *New Tricks*, discovered that her mother had a half-brother called Cyril, who had been the illegitimate son of their mother, Agnes, born before she married Amanda's grandfather. Amanda managed to piece together the puzzle of what happened to Cyril by discussing the subject with family members, and that remains the best way to find out more about illegitimate ancestors. Other methods to solve the riddle of illegitimate ancestors include examining marriage indexes for the months after the birth, to see if mother and father married, by force or by choice, to hide their shame. BMDs and the census are the main tools, but don't be afraid to look at parish records, too. Baptism records can be revealing. It was not unusual for an illegitimate child to be labelled as a 'bastard' on baptism registers, which was hardly the sort of thing entered on birth certificates! For further background and research tips, it is worth consulting *My Ancestor Was a Bastard* by Sarah Paley (Society of Genealogists, 2011).

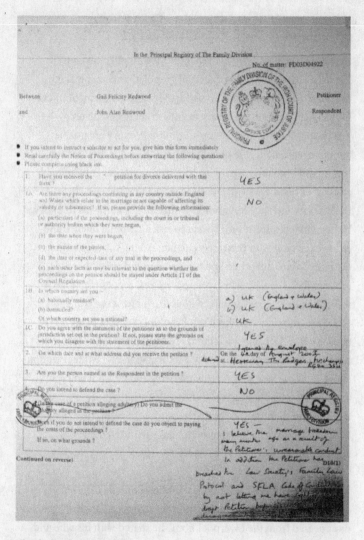

In the Principal Registry of The Family Division

No. of matter: FD03D04922

Between   Gail Felicity Redwood   Petitioner

and   John Alan Redwood   Respondent

- If you intend to instruct a solicitor to act for you, give him this form immediately
- Read carefully the Notice of Proceedings before answering the following questions
- Please complete using black ink

1. Have you received the ___ petition for divorce delivered with this form ?	YES
1A. Are there any proceedings continuing in any country outside England and Wales which relate to the marriage or are capable of affecting its validity or subsistence? If so, please provide the following information: (a) particulars of the proceedings, including the court in or tribunal or authority before which they were begun, (b) the date when they were begun, (c) the names of the parties, (d) the date or expected date of any trial in the proceedings, and (e) such other facts as may be relevant to the question whether the proceedings on the petition should be stayed under Article 11 of the Council Regulation	NO
1B. In which country are you – (a) habitually resident? (b) domiciled? Of which country are you a national?	a) UK (England + Wales) b) UK (England + Wales) UK
1C. Do you agree with the statement of the petitioner as to the grounds of jurisdiction set out in the petition? If not, please state the grounds on which you disagree with the statement of the petitioner.	YES
2. On which date and at what address did you receive the petition ?	On the 2nd day of August 2003 ... opened by envelope ... st. Herewian The Rodges. Wokingham RG22 3SU
3. Are you the person named as the Respondent in the petition ?	YES
4. Do you intend to defend the case ?	NO
5. (In the case of a petition alleging adultery) Do you admit the adultery alleged in the petition?	
6. (In the case if you do not intend to defend the case do you object to paying the costs of the proceedings ? If so, on what grounds ?	YES – I believe the marriage broke down many months ago as a result of the Petitioner's unreasonable conduct. In addition the Petitioner has breached the Law Society's Family Law Protocol and SFLA Code of Conduct by not letting me have a draft Petition before ...

Continued on reverse)

D10(1)

The divorce papers of John
Redwood M.P. and Gail Redwood.
Unreasonable behaviour was cited
as the reason for divorce.

Bigamy and Divorce

In the first series of *Who Do You Think You Are?*, comedian Vic Reeves discovered that his maternal grandfather, Simeon Leigh, had married twice without divorcing. His case is not uncommon. In the late nineteenth and early twentieth centuries, divorce was the privilege of the wealthy. Ordinary people were unable to obtain legal aid for divorce cases until the 1920s. Before then, incompatible couples separated and lived apart, either by mutual consent or because one party left to start a new life elsewhere. As the years passed they might meet someone else and wish to marry. Understandably, some didn't want to risk a criminal offence and chose to cohabit with their new partner, risking the accusation of 'living in sin'. But others took the plunge and risked possible prosecution. Then, of course, there were real rogues who married more than one person and lived double lives (or even triple for the more ambitious!) without their multiple spouses being aware of each other. How can you find these bigamists? They will have been practised liars who gave false information on civil registration entries and parish registers to avoid being caught, so if you spot any discrepancies between documents for a certain person you might be on their trail. If they were caught, it is well worth getting hold of local newspapers that might have reported their trial and conviction.

In her episode, Kim Cattrall, star of *Sex and the City*, set off in pursuit of her maternal grandfather, George Baugh, who disappeared from the Liverpool home he shared with his wife and three daughters, including Kim's mum, in 1938. George, somewhat brazenly, started a second family just north of the city as his first family slid into poverty. It was that fact and the scars it left on her mother, rather than the mere fact of his bigamy, which shocked Kim.

She told the camera she would never be able to forgive him for what he had done.

As mentioned above, bigamy was a problem because divorces were so hard to come by. It was also much harder for women to divorce than men. To obtain a divorce, all a man had to do was prove adultery, whereas a woman had to prove that her husband's infidelity was accompanied by either violence or desertion!

If your ancestors were wealthy enough to afford a divorce before 1938 (files from 1938 onwards have mostly been destroyed) then it's worth checking with the Principal Registry of the Family Division in London, which has a central index for all divorce suits from 1858. Thousands of cases between 1858 and 1911 are available on www. ancestry.co.uk (subject to a subscription fee), and these not only give the names of the parties involved but also list the history of the marriage and often include the details of the alleged wrongdoing which prompted the divorce. Both prior to and after 1938, it's worth checking local and national newspapers because divorce cases were a common source of scandalous copy for eager hacks and salacious editors. Divorce case files up to 1938 are available at The National Archives and can be searched by name at www.nationalarchives.gov. uk/records/looking-for-person/divorce.html.

Criminal Ancestors

For all scandal hunters, the holy grail is a criminal ancestor. Former footballer Gary Lineker delved deep into his family's history and unearthed the tale of James Pratt, his great-great-great-grandfather. James was a poacher and spent much of the 1840s in and out of Leicester prison. A bad egg? Once Gary learned more about his ancestor's circumstances, he didn't think so. James had eight children, times were tough, so he resorted to stealing to try and feed them. It was not successful – two of the kids died before the age of one. Gary was not the only celebrity to discover a criminal in his ancestral closet. Opera singer Lesley Garrett discovered her great-great-grandfather poisoned his wife with carbolic acid. What's more, he got away with it.

If you encounter a criminal ancestor, the best place to start are court records. Depending on the court, which in turn depends on the severity of the crime, the places to look are either your local record office or the National Archives. Quarter session, petty sessions or magistrate's court records, if they exist, will be at your local archive or record office. The records of assize courts, where most trials were held, are at the National Archives, including indictments, which give the nature of the charge as well as the defendant's details and some depositions, and witness statements taken ahead of the trial (though few of those survive after 1830).

A great online resource, though subject to a subscription fee, is the searchable criminal registers held by www.ancestry.co.uk. These cover the dates 1791–1892 and include biographical information about the criminals, as well as the crime, the date and place where they were tried, their sentences, where they were served and their date of release (or execution, for the gravest crimes). This information can lead you to other records for more information, such as court records, prison registers (held in local record offices prior to 1877 and the National Archives thereafter), Calendar of Prisoners (also held at the National Archives, although you'll need to know the prison or county where your ancestor was held to search these effectively) and even transportation records.

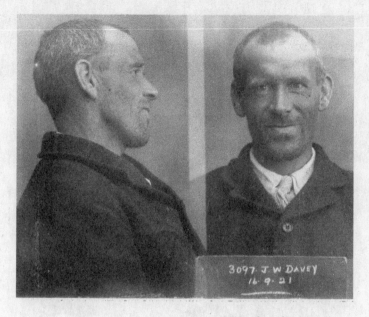

A mug shot of Osip
Mandelstam (1891-1938).

Finally, often the best resource of all are local newspapers, which had a reporter stationed in each court and filled their pages with accounts of even the most minor case. Your local library should have back copies of the local newspaper, either in bound copies or microfilm form. The British Library's Newspaper Archive in Colindale has closed and its collection, at the time of writing, was being moved. Print newspapers will be available from the library from autumn 2014. As for online searches, it is worth checking out www.britishnewspaperarchive.co.uk, a project to digitize up to 40 million newspaper pages in the next ten years. At the time of writing, almost 7.5 million pages were online: a vast amount, although the project is still a long way from being complete.

AINSLEY HARRIOTT

Like many of us, TV chef and presenter Ainsley's main motivation for researching his family history was the prospect of discovery. 'It's like reading a new book for the first time,' he told the camera. 'You turn the pages and you don't know what you're going to discover.' Ainsley wasn't to know that his particular book would be a thriller, teeming with mystery and twists.

AS ALL GOOD researchers do, he began at home with his sister Jackie. His parents had separated in 1965 and Ainsley never felt he had the time or opportunity to learn much about his father's line and the Harriott name. Jackie had already researched Ainsley's maternal line and he hoped she might lift the fog that surrounded his father's ancestry. She told him that Chester Harriott was born in Kingston, Jamaica, in 1932, the son of Oscar and Mina Love Harriott, and there was a family rumour that Chester's grandmother had been born in Bombay, India. In pursuit of the truth, Ainsley travelled to Jamaica on what became an emotional Caribbean odyssey.

* * *

There he was told by an aunt that his great-grandmother, Alide Maude Hibbert, was born in Calcutta rather than Bombay, but Ainsley noted that her name hardly suggested any Indian roots. His suspicions were proved right when he visited the Jamaican records office and learned that she had been born in Jamaica, as had her parents. The Indian heritage story was a family myth. But he did discover that Alide's grandmother, Catherine Smith, had lived on the island before slavery was abolished in 1838. Her baptism records described her as 'mulatto': mixed race. Her father, John Briggs, had been a white overseer at Wear Penn and one of his roles, it seems likely, was to produce as many children as possible to help replenish the slave stock. Briggs had many children and one was Catherine Smith, born to Joan Davy (bearing the name of her slave owner, John Davy).

It was an 'eye-opening' revelation for Ainsley. The treatment of his ancestors, and the discovery that one of them was a white man who forced himself on a black slave was unsettling. He had been prepared for some unpleasant facts, but the truth was more disconcerting than he anticipated. His discomfort was not to end there.

He returned to the Harriott line to learn more about his great-grandfather, Ebeneezer Harriott, a decorated hero of the West India Regiment at the turn of the twentieth century. He fought in several conflicts across the world, making his name in the bloody 'Hut Tax Affair' conflict in Sierra Leone, where he rose, to Ainsley's obvious pride, from a lowly corporal to sergeant. His wife was Constance Walrond, son of John and Irenea Walrond. Following their lineage in the archives in Barbados, Ainsley discovered that Irenea's father, James E. Hunte, was a policeman shortly after emancipation. As the police force was founded to 'protect' white settlers from newly freed slaves, it seemed likely that James Hunte was a free man before slavery was abolished. The records confirmed it. His mother, Rachel, was listed as a 'free negro'. It also turned out that her son, James, owned nine properties. Ainsley was intrigued. A local historian, Pedro Walsh, supplied some possible answers. The properties were in the city's red-light district. There was a good chance Rachel built up some personal wealth from prostitution and passed it to her son, a policeman. Rather than being shocked, Ainsley was moved. These were difficult times. People did what they could to survive and Rachel had proved remarkably successful.

The final leg of Ainsley's quest was answering the question of where the Harriott name came from. He went back to the Jamaica archives to search for more information about his great-grandfather, Ebeneezer. On the International Genealogical Index website (now

Ebeneezer Harriott,
Ainsley's great-grandfather.

renamed as Family Search) he found record of his baptism in 1865. His father was James Gordon Harriott. More research uncovered an astonishing secret – James had been white. Even more amazingly, he had been a slave owner.

Ainsley was left speechless. Earlier on his journey he had been profoundly angered by the treatment of his slave ancestors. Now he was having to digest the fact that one line of his ancestry, the very one that gave him his name, had owned slaves. The programme

Ainsley's paternal grandparents,
Oscar and Mina Love Harriott, on
their wedding day.

ended with Ainsley touring the plantation and abandoned house
where James Harriott had lived. His emotions were difficult to
sum up, but Ainsley had encountered a truth about family history:
sometimes what we find is unpalatable, but it's a chapter in our
family story. Or, as Ainsley put it: 'Good or bad, it's part of my
make-up.'

DURING THE WAR.

o, each soldier.)

ginal when corresponding with a

prenticeship has been interrupted
ny employment in a trade similar
g such Military Service.

L/Cpl

TT

5 - 23 Res Bn

Period.

To *14 . 9 . 18 .*

18   2   1   9 .

nt 6 . 1. 19 to 18 . 4 . 19

"

shown in A. B. 64).

man (Innr)

in Active Service Army

Priers Heath

Priers Heath

WAR
STORIES

WAR STORIES

Almost everyone who searches through their family's past will find an ancestor who fought in a war or served king and country as a member of the armed forces. The twentieth century was marked by the two most cataclysmic conflicts in history and both touched our ancestors' lives. Thankfully, for the past few centuries or so, the armed forces have been excellent record-keepers, so if you have military ancestors there's a good chance you'll find some mention of them, ranging from their service records, to their pay and pensions and whether they were decorated as heroes.

***

Following the quest for a military ancestor can be one of the most absorbing aspects of family history. Knowing they risked their lives in some of history's greatest and most notorious battles is also deeply humbling. Through information obtained from his family, the impressionist and comedian Rory Bremner was able to find his father's military service record, where he learned that he had landed in Normandy 23 days after D-Day. His father's regiment museum was able to put Rory in touch with historians who told him what his father might have experienced during that campaign, and eventually he found a revealing, and moving, eye-witness account from a Dutch civilian who had been alongside Major Bremner in battle. This gave Rory detailed knowledge of his father's experiences and reactions in the heat of battle.

The steps Rory took are good ones to remember. Start at home with any information from relatives. Use this to track down a service record or other records that reveal the details of your ancestor's military career. Approach any museum of the regiment your ancestor belonged to and see what help, records or information they can provide. They might have accounts written by people who served at the same time as your ancestor, which would offer colour and detail about any campaigns or conflict they saw. Then, if relevant, and if time and expense allow, a visit to the site where your ancestor saw action is a fascinating, and often emotional, way to end your journey. In the first series of *Who Do You Think You Are?*, Ian Hislop did just that, visiting the site of the Battle of Spion Kop, where hundreds of British soldiers were killed trying to hold a hill in the Boer War. Ian's grandfather, William Beddows of the Royal Lancasters, was one of the lucky ones who survived.

A quick word of reassurance here: tracing a military ancestor can seem very daunting, given the diverse information available, but with patience and time, and the confidence to ask for help from archive and museum staff, it can be extremely rewarding. The National Archives in Kew is an excellent resource for tracing military ancestry. The staff there will only be too willing to point you in the right direction. But an increasing amount of records can also be found online, though you may have to pay to access them.

The Army Game

Prior to the English Civil War, there was no regular British army. Kings, earls, barons, or whichever landed gent had enough spare cash raised their own militias of local men to fight on behalf of their interests. With the restoration of Charles II to the throne in 1660, the decision was taken to create a standing army to defend the crown. Those regiments were the first of what has become the modern

British Army. Indeed, the regimental structure has been the basis for the army ever since, grouped into four categories:

- **CAVALRY:** Troops mounted on horseback, although after the carnage of the First World War, horses were replaced by tanks.
- **ARTILLERY:** Troops specially trained to use heavy guns.
- **ENGINEERS:** Troops trained to provide engineering and other support to front-line troops. For example, construction projects such as bridge-building.
- **INFANTRY:** Troops of foot soldiers who traditionally form the bulk of the armed forces and served on the front line in conflict.

Over time, regiments have come and gone, merged and been renamed. But thankfully the Internet is a researcher's friend; it is possible to type a regiment name into a search engine and discover if it still exists, whether it has a website and museum, or whether it merged with another or was disbanded, and if so what happened to it. Knowing your ancestor's regiment is essential to learning about their military career, as the army did not have a central record-keeping system until the First World War.

It's equally important to know the rank of your ancestor. Up until the First World War, officers were drawn almost exclusively from the wealthy elite. Their records can be found on the Army List, which lists officers by name and gives details of promotions, units served with and other information. For the common soldier, service records are the best place to start – these are indexed by regiment – and muster rolls, which provide details of pay, any offences they might have committed and the location of their regiment. Medal rolls are also worth consulting if you believe your ancestor was decorated for their service. Many of these records are held at the National Archives: www.nationalarchives.gov.uk/battles/ancestors/army.htm.

Military Rank: the Army

For the uninitiated, it can be confusing to work out
where your ancestor fitted into the army's unique
structure. Here's a list, from smallest to largest, of how
the army was divided:

- Soldier
- Platoon
- Company
- Regiment
- Brigade
- Division
- Corps

Ranks

The rank system forms the backbone of the army's
structure. Here's the system from lowest to highest, so
you can see how high your ancestor rose:

- Private
- Lance Corporal
- Corporal
- Sergeant
- Staff/Colour
  Sergeant
- Sergeant Major
- Second Lieutenant
  (lowest officer rank)
- Lieutenant
- Captain
- Major
- Lieutenant Colonel
- Colonel
- Brigadier
- Major General
- Lieutenant General
- General
- Field Marshal

In the Navy

A navy of sorts has defended Britain's shores since the ninth century, but it was only in 1660 that it became the Royal Navy, the ferocious, feared fighting force of legend. In the same way that knowing your army ancestor's regiment helps to track down their records, it is useful to know the name of the ships your naval forebear sailed on, especially for the common sailor. Then you can try to track down his muster roll, which offers details of service and pay, as well as the ship's logbook, which can provide intriguing details of a ship's voyages as well as passing references to your ancestor and his fellow crew. If they were officer class, the Navy List offers similar details to the Army List. Again, the National Archives is a good port of call for finding naval ancestors, as well as the National Maritime Museum. Both offer several research guides outlining the information in their archives.

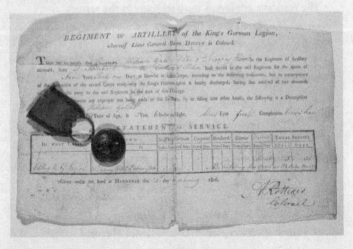

Unclaimed Waterloo campaign medal awarded to Driver William Gallas, King's German Artillary, with his discharge papers, 1815.

The National Archives has also put 600,000 Royal Navy service records online for those sailors who joined between 1853 and 1923. It is an excellent resource. There are also searchable databases for Royal Navy officers' service records 1756–1931 and Royal Navy service records 1756–1931. You can find out more (together with more online naval databases) at www.nationalarchives.gov.uk/records/navy.htm.

Military Rank: the Navy

Here are the ranks of the navy from lowest to highest:

- Able Seaman
- Leading Seaman
- Petty Officer
- Chief Petty Officer
- Warrant Officer
- Midshipman (lowest officer rank)
- Sub-lieutenant
- Lieutenant
- Lieutenant Commander
- Commander
- Captain
- Commodore
- Rear Admiral
- Vice Admiral
- Admiral
- Admiral of the Fleet

Lewis machine gunners, Hollebeke, Belgium, World War 1, 1914-1918. Belgian soldiers pose with British Tommies at the junction of the Belgian and British lines.

First World War

There are very few lives that weren't touched by what H. G. Wells called 'the war that will end war'. Most of us will have ancestors who were among the estimated nine million men and women who served, or one of the 723,000 British servicemen who were killed and the million-plus who were wounded. The National Archives has a mass of material to enable you to find out more.

Army

There are three main sources of information to find out more about your ancestor's wartime adventures.

- **SERVICE RECORDS:** Unfortunately, more than half of these were destroyed during the Blitz in 1940. However, roughly 40 per cent survived, so there is a chance you might be able to find your ancestor in there. If you are lucky, you'll find the date of their enlistment and details of any wounds or injuries, although the information can vary. Many of them are available to view at www.ancestry.co.uk.

- **MEDAL ROLLS:** If your ancestor was awarded a medal for their service – and every soldier of the First World War was given two campaign medals: the British War Medal and the Victory Medal – then it was recorded in medal rolls and given an index card. The National Archives has almost five million of these index cards and, helpfully, it has made them available online. For each person, the card records name, rank, unit, regimental number and medal entitlement. Often there is information about when and where your ancestor first entered the war and, occasionally, either their date of death, date of discharge or other remarks concerning their career or fate. You can search at www.nationalarchives.gov.uk/records/medal-index-cards-ww1.htm.

- **WAR DIARIES:** If you know the regiment to which your ancestor was attached, it's worth finding their war diaries. While these are unlikely to mention your ancestor by name, they are contemporaneous accounts of that unit's operational life and provide a wonderful feel for the life your ancestor lived, as well as describing the action they saw, often in vivid detail. You can search them by regiment, battalion, brigade or division at www. nationalarchives.gov.uk/records/war-diaries-ww1.htm?WT.ac=-.

Navy

Using the service records above, as well as the Navy List for officers, it is possible to discover more information about the role of your naval ancestors in the Great War. But be aware that the conflict was primarily fought on land and the navy saw comparatively little action. Like their army counterparts, medal rolls are a useful way of tracking your naval ancestors in war, and ancestry.co.uk has a searchable index between 1793 and 1949. A subscription fee is required to view the results.

Royal Air Force

The Royal Air Force (RAF) was formed in 1918, combining the Royal Flying Corps (RFC) and Royal Naval Air Service (RNAS). For details of the RFC you can check army records, and for the RNAS check the navy records. Service records 1918–1922 are available at the National Archives, as well as officer records and officer lists. Findmypast.co.uk has the only complete muster roll of the RAF of 1918, from which you can find out your ancestor's role in the RAF, their rank, date and term of enlistment and even rate of pay.

US troops climbing over barbed wire barriers in their attack against German positions, 1918.

Military Ranks: the RAF

Here are the ranks of the RAF from lowest to highest:

- Aircraftman
- Leading Aircraftman
- Senior Aircraftman
- Corporal
- Sergeant
- Flight Sergeant
- Warrant Officer
- Pilot Officer (lowest officer rank)
- Flying Officer
- Flight Lieutenant
- Squadron Leader
- Wing Commander
- Group Captain
- Air Commodore
- Air Vice-Marshal
- Air Marshal
- Air Chief Marshal
- Marshal of the Royal Air Force

Second World War

Surviving service records for those who fought in the second great conflict of the twentieth century are not yet in the public domain because they are still retained by the Ministry of Defence, although next of kin can apply directly to the Ministry to see them. See www.gov.uk/requests-for-personal-data-and-service-records.

There are yet more ways one can search for information about a Second World War ancestor. If you know your ancestor was killed in service, you can check the Army Roll of Honour, which will give details of their date of death, rank, the regiment they served with and the theatre of war in which they served. If they were captured, consult the British Army Prisoners of War 1939–45, where you can discover your ancestor's rank, regiment, prison number and where they were held. Both of these databases can be searched at www.ancestry.co.uk.

The National Archives also has copies of unit war diaries, which, if you know the theatre of war your ancestor was fighting in and their unit name, will give you a daily record of their operations. It is also worth checking the collection at the Imperial War Museum, which has almost 18,000 private papers, mainly unpublished diaries, letters and memoirs written by servicemen since 1914. You can find more information at www.iwm.org.uk

War on the Web

There are many websites which offer a range of searchable military records, and some have already been mentioned in this section. Here are two more useful sites that might be able to help you trace your military ancestors.

- **www.cwgc.org** is the website of the Commonwealth War Graves Commission, a crucial resource that ensures the 1.7 million men and women who died in the two world wars will not be forgotten. They offer a searchable database of graves and memorials in 153 countries. You can find your ancestor's rank, date of death, age, regiment, and the precise location of his or her grave should you wish to visit it.
- **www.forces-war-records.co.uk** offers a vast range of military records, almost five million at the time of writing, dating back to the Napoleonic Wars. Subscription at the time of writing was £8.65 a month or £85.95 a year.

ALAN CUMMING

Sometimes there's a person in our family's past whose story intrigues us more than anybody else's. This was the case for Scottish-born actor Alan Cumming. Like many of us, he didn't know much about his family beyond the living. But the story of his maternal grandfather, Tom Darling, was a family mystery – 'The Black Hole', as Alan referred to it. He had fought in the Second World War, rarely came back to his wife and children and died in a shooting accident.

ALAN WENT BACK to see his mother in Dundee
feeling a 'bit like Miss Marple' to gather as many clues as possible
to start his quest for Tom Darling. She told him the story they
had heard was that Tom had been killed when he was cleaning his
gun and it fired by accident.

* * *

Tom had been born in 1916. He joined the vaunted Cameron
Highlanders regiment, a close-knit unit of men famous for their
courage and loyalty to each other. In 1937 he married Margaret,
Alan's beloved granny. A year later Alan's mum, Mary, was born, to
be followed by two more children. In the meantime, Tom had made
his way from being a cook to a motor mechanic in the Highlanders.
His talent for motorbike riding earned him the position of despatch
rider, transferring messages between HQ and the front line.

In May 1940, after the outbreak of the Second World War, the
Highlanders were engaged near La Bassée trying to hold back the
German forces so the Allies could escape from Dunkirk. In one
battle they fought gamely against Rommel and his advancing tanks.
As the sky rained fire and fury, Tom Darling rode to and from the
front line on his motorbike laden with ammunition to make sure
his comrades were well stocked for the fight. For his extraordinary
bravery in the most perilous of circumstances he was awarded a
Gallantry Medal. He was a hero.

Yet Alan could not help but wonder whether his experiences

*Alan's maternal grandparents,
Tom and Mary Darling, on their
wedding day.*

that day might have contributed to 'the end of the story' and Tom's violent death. In London he met with Professor Edgar Jones, historian and expert in military psychiatry, to explore how Tom's experiences might have affected his mental health. In 1942 Tom was sent with the Highlanders to India for jungle training. Two years later he fought in the notorious Battle of Kohima against the ferocious, committed Japanese army where he was wounded in action. His record, kept by Alan's mother, showed that he was treated in a military hospital for several months before he was transferred to another hospital in Deolali, India, 1,000 miles away. That place is where the word 'doolally' (meaning mad or eccentric) stems from. The official record of his service has a gap where this part of his military career should be. Professor Jones told Alan that after the war, because of the stigma attached to mental illness, many pages of records belonging to soldiers who had experienced major psychiatric episodes had been destroyed. Therefore there was a good chance that Tom had suffered some kind of mental illness.

Alan travelled to Bristol to meet a veteran of the Battle of Kohima, David Murray, who also knew his grandfather and respected him greatly. He gave a vivid description of that brutal, bloody battle, where more than 100 out of 400 men were killed, wounded or went missing. Tom had been wounded and it would have been no surprise if his experiences had left him traumatized. Alan told the camera he was now getting a sense of Tom as a person and not a 'bravery machine'.

Directly after the war, Tom returned home to see his family. But he soon left. They would never see him again. After a stint in the army, then a period as a sales clerk in St Albans, he applied for a post as a policeman in Malaya. In 1948 communist guerrillas had started a bloody campaign against their colonial masters. It was Tom's job to help keep the peace in the new villages that had been built to house the local population – and isolate them from the rebels.

Seven months after arriving in Malaya he was dead. Alan travelled to Kuala Lumpur, now the capital of Malaysia, to find out more. His death certificate confirmed that he had died of a gunshot wound. But the autopsy report said that the wound was to the back of his head, which, as Alan noted, ruled out the theory of it being a cleaning accident.

*Tom Darling,
Alan's maternal
grandfather.*

Tom had been stationed in Chaah. Alan visited the village where
he met an ex-colleague of Tom's. To his immense shock, he learned
that Tom had been killed playing a game of Russian roulette for
money. 'What state of mind must he have been in?' Alan wondered.
Alan returned to the capital where he read official confirmation that
Tom had died in a deadly game. But crucially, this detail was omitted
from the letter sent to Alan's granny notifying her of her husband's
death. Instead it referred to an accident – hence the story the family
had subsequently told.

It was the end of a remarkable journey, but one Alan was glad to
have taken. It underlined his belief that it was best to be honest and
open and not cover up any uncomfortable secrets. 'The truth can
hurt,' he said, 'but not knowing can hurt more.'

PATRICK STEWART

It was only in recent years that actor Patrick Stewart became aware he had been 'channelling' his father in a variety of his theatre roles 'for years and years'. 'I want to understand that,' he told the camera. He and his family, it would be fair to say, endured a difficult relationship with Alfred Stewart before his death in 1980. Patrick remembers him as an angry figure, who often took that anger out on their mother, Gladys. His father had told him some stories of his time in the military but there was much more Patrick wanted to know about his service. Perhaps it might help him better understand his father and his actions?

HIS FIRST STOP was the Imperial War Museum in London, where he learned from his service record that Alfred had enlisted in the army just over two weeks after Patrick's eldest brother Geoffrey had been born. Patrick knew that Geoffrey was born out of wedlock and that his mother and father didn't marry until 1933, when Geoffrey was eight. This suggested that joining the army was some kind of escape.

* * *

Whatever his reasons for joining, Alfred found army life to his liking. He joined the Regimental Police (RP), overseeing the men's behaviour and guarding those imprisoned for offences. The RP had power and were feared by the ranks, a position for which Patrick felt his father was well suited.

Once his service was over he returned to Mirfield, West Yorkshire, and married Gladys. But at the outbreak of the Second World War he was recalled and assigned to the King's Own Yorkshire Light Infantry (KOYLI). These were an untrained group of men designated to play a support role behind front-line forces. A man of Alfred's experience and authority would have been able to offer them ad hoc training and act as a mentor.

They left for France in the spring of 1940, expecting to dig railways and build bridges to serve the main force. But the rapid German invasion of France caught the Allied forces by surprise and, unexpectedly and hastily, the KOYLI were called into action

Patrick (far right) with his mother, Gladys,
(centre) and brother Trevor (far left).

to try and hold up the German offensive, although given their lack of training it was unlikely that they would be more than a minor obstacle. Alfred and the rest of his battalion were sent by train towards the Belgian border, but came to a halt outside Abbeville. A crack Panzer division was laying waste to the town by land and air and the men were forced to get off the train and shelter in a nearby field. They saw hundreds of refugees fleeing the destruction and were forced to retreat to safety, under intense fire, passing bombed-out trains and corpses on their way. It must have been a hellish experience, especially for a unit that had barely seen action before. Alfred eventually made it out of France, one of the last groups of British troops to be evacuated.

On his return, Alfred was the subject of a story in the local gazette. Patrick was shocked to read his father's vivid description of the horrific sights he'd witnessed in France, but even more stunned to discover that his father admitted to having shellshock, 'from which he still suffers', the report added. Patrick wondered if it might explain the angry man of his childhood. 'I'm seeing a story here now,' he said. It wasn't simply the story of his father's service, fascinating though that was, but a psychological narrative.

Regardless of his experiences, Alfred soon rejoined the conflict. Despite being in his late thirties, he joined the newly founded Parachute Regiment as sergeant. He took part in Operation Dragoon in 1944, one of the most successful Allied operations of the Second World War, parachuting into southern France to secure a pocket of land ahead of a naval invasion. Patrick visited the place where his father landed, saw the site where he and others secured and protected a headquarters, and spoke to local people who still remembered the day of their liberation. But Alfred's remarkable military story didn't end there. During the battle at Arnhem, the 2nd Battalion, Parachute Regiment had been decimated. In January, Alfred was made its sergeant-major, tasked with helping to restore the troops' morale and confidence after their devastating losses. The irony of him acting as a father figure to his men, when he was not much of a father to his own children, was not lost on Patrick.

The next step on his quest was to investigate his brother Geoffrey's belief that Alfred was not his real father. In the Wakefield Registry of Deeds, he found court records of a 'bastardy application' made by his mother only months after Geoffrey had been born. She succeeded in proving Alfred was the father and the court ordered him to pay ten shillings a week for his son's upkeep. It must have taken great courage for Gladys to stand up in court, face Alfred and risk the public shame and stigma of illegitimacy in order to make sure that her son was provided for.

Patrick's father, Alfred Stewart.

Patrick ended his quest with a meeting with his brother Trevor to share his findings. He had done more research into shellshock and learned of the isolation their father might have felt, as well as the possible nightmares and flashbacks. It was not uncommon for sufferers to turn to drink or become involved in crime or domestic violence. Both Trevor and Patrick agreed that this information shed new light on a complicated man. Patrick told the camera he was 'warming' to his father. 'It doesn't in any way affect my feelings about domestic violence, or that what he did was wrong, but now there are other elements in it, and it's those other elements I've found so compelling and beautiful.'

TOIL AND
HARD GRAFT

TOIL AND HARD GRAFT

For the vast majority of our ancestors, work was a daily grind: long hours, low pay, often in hazardous conditions. It depended on the industry or profession, but it was common for a working day to begin around 6am and to go on until 5.30pm or later. In some industries people worked weekends, too, while holidays were non-existent. For many, it was a tedious, tiring grind, but their existence depended on it. When we research our family history we tend to focus on the milestones of our ancestors' lives: their births, marriages and deaths in particular. Along with the census, these offer a snapshot of their lives. But by researching their occupations we can discover the detail and reality of their daily existence.

* * *

The best sources for ascertaining your ancestor's occupation are marriage and death certificates and census returns. The census allows you to track the progress, if any, of your ancestor's career over a period of time or follow any changes in occupation. There's a good chance you might encounter some archaic job titles you're not familiar with, or trades and professions that have subsequently died out (see box). In 100 years time it may be that our predecessors will be looking at census returns and scratching their heads about what a 'Consultant' or 'IT Director' is.

Through her family, Jodie Kidd learned that her great-grandfather, Rowland Frederick Hodge, had been involved in shipbuilding in Newcastle, then at the heart of the country's thriving shipping industry. In the 1881 census he was registered as a clerk;

ten years later he was manager of a shipbuilding firm; a decade, later he owned his own company. After checking the census records, it was time to turn to guilds and trade organizations, in this case Trinity House, which has kept records of shipping and seafaring in Newcastle for centuries. There Jodie found a biography of significant people in the industry, which included her great-grandfather. It revealed that he founded a shipping company, and through a local, specialist historian she was able to learn more about her ancestor's successful career. He rose to such prominence that in 1921 he was made a baronet.

It is a good template for a family historian to follow. Start with census returns, which lead to specialist archives or trade organizations, which often boast expert staff who can guide you to the right place in their collections, and then a specialist or local historian. Often the archive or organization you have contacted will know someone, or you can get in touch with your local library or museum to see if they can recommend someone to help. Jodie's ancestor became a man of wealth and standing so it was easier for her to learn about him than a lowly riveter, for example. But even if your ancestors did not rise beyond the shop floor, trade organizations and archives can give you a glimpse of what their working life would have been like and put flesh on their bones.

Specialized Industries

It would take several volumes to address every single trade or industry your ancestors might have worked in, but here are a few of the more common ones you might encounter in your research, with advice on where to find more information. Public servants like police officers and firefighters, and professions such as doctors and lawyers, were generally well recorded, but it is possible to find information about those in less-heralded lines of work.

Farming

Virtually everybody who traces their ancestry back to the early nineteenth century will come across ancestors who worked on the land. In the 1851 census, almost 1.5 million people were recorded as agricultural labourers or similar. There's very little information available about these people, but the Museum of English Rural Life is a good place to start (www.reading.ac.uk/merl/). There you can find photographs, books, journals and pamphlets that offer a fascinating insight into life in farming communities.

Domestic Service

Although agricultural labourer was the most common job in 1851, by 1871 it had been replaced by domestic service. By the end of the Victorian era, it wasn't just the Downton Abbeys that had staff. The members of the emerging middle class were status-conscious and keen to enjoy the fruits of their labour by employing servants. The census is the prime resource for finding out whom your ancestors worked for and where. Excellent resources for learning more about life below stairs are: *My Ancestor Was a Domestic Servant* by Pamela Horn (Society of Genealogists, 2009) and *Tracing Your Servant Ancestors* by Michelle Higgs (Pen & Sword Family History, 2012).

Coal Mining

The Industrial Revolution was powered by steam. Much of that steam was produced from coal dug out by hundreds of thousands of men who worked miles below ground, performing some of the most dangerous and backbreaking work known to man. The National Coal Mining Museum in Wakefield (www.ncm.org.uk) gives a wonderful flavour of what life was like underground for our

*Women sorting wool in an early
blanket factory in Witney,
Oxforshire, 1860-1922.*

coal-mining ancestors. You can travel 450 feet down to the coalface,
as Lesley Garrett did in her episode of *Who Do You Think You Are?*
while researching her great-grandfather, to gain a first-hand glimpse
of the cramped conditions and get a feel for the dust and noise and
danger. *My Ancestor Was a Coalminer* by David Tonks (Society
of Genealogists, 2010) also offers an exhaustive directory of local
archives, libraries and museums that can tell you more about your
ancestors and the pits they worked in.

Merchant Navy

As an island race the British have always worked on the sea, and
during the age of Empire thousands worked on ships ferrying
goods to and from far-flung parts of the globe. From 1835, the
merchant navy was regulated by the Board of Trade, which is good
news for genealogists because it means there are records. TNA has
a wealth of resources, including crew lists and officer service records.

A good online port of call is Findmypast.co.uk, which has an index of 270,000 merchant seamen on their site, taken from crew lists between 1861 and 1913. If your ancestor worked in the merchant navy after 1917, the National Archives has the Central Indexed Register of Merchant Seamen 1918–41. Learn more at www.nationalarchives.gov.uk/records/looking-for-person/merchantseamanafter1917.htm. FindMyPast also has the same register available online for subscribers.

The 'My Ancestor' series of books, mentioned above and published by the Society of Genealogists, are excellent guides for researching your ancestors' occupations, and cover a wide range of trades and professions, including lawyers, railway workers, the clergy, even studio photographers! More information can be found at www.sog.org.uk.

Trading Places

The trades and professions mentioned above are only a few of the thousands of different jobs our ancestors might have performed. Just as we'll nearly always come across an agricultural labourer or domestic servant in our family tree, we'll also come across those who started their own business or were self-employed; perhaps they owned or ran a pub or a shop, or were tradesmen such as cobblers or blacksmiths. If you discover these occupations from certificates or census returns, it's worth checking local trade directories of the time, which were compiled annually and can tell you where your ancestors had premises, any business partners they might have had and even who their business rivals were in the area!

There are 675 trade directories available to search online at www. historicaldirectories.org, including at least one directory for every English and Welsh county for each of the 1850s, 1890s and 1910s. If your ancestors owned a business, it's also worth checking through old copies of the local newspaper to see if there are any stories about them or advertisements they might have placed, as well as contacting any local history groups who might have collected reminiscences and photographs that include your ancestor's business. The local studies section of your nearest library is another potential source of information.

A British soldier's certificate of employment during the war, 18 April 1919. This document was designed to assist soldiers in finding work after the war.

Circa 1900: Women having this dinner in a
a workhouse in St Pancras, London.

The Shadow of the Workhouse

For those who couldn't find or were unable to work, then life before, during and even after Victorian Britain could be brutal. Poverty and slum housing, and the illness and mortality that accompanied it, were a fact of life for many of our ancestors. As you scroll through census returns, there's a good chance you'll find ancestors who fell on hard times, and there was no welfare state to act as a safety net. Before 1834 the poor were at the mercy of their local parish for relief, until the Poor Law Amendment Act of 1834 abandoned that system and grouped parishes into unions to oversee workhouses. These institutions were made as harsh and unattractive as possible to act as a deterrent to all but the truly destitute, and great stigma was attached to ending up in one. Those inmates who didn't conform to the strict rules were ordered to perform hard labour – much like a prison, except that their only crime was being poor.

Strictly Come Dancing judge Len Goodman, who memorably said his younger self couldn't give a 'monkey's armpit' about genealogy, learned during his journey into his family's past of some ancestors who were sent to one of these notorious places. The Bethnal Green Workhouse had only two paid nurses, both untrained, to treat up to 100 sick men and women and no running water available between 5pm and 7am. For many, the shame was as difficult to cope with as the hardship. Len's ancestor, John Cecil, had once been a silk weaver but had been forced into the workhouse after sliding into poverty. He died in there of asthma. Twenty years later and Len's great-great-grandfather faced a similar prospect. Rather than go into the workhouse where his father had died, he chose to hang himself, aged 69.

If you discover that your ancestors were sent to a workhouse, there are a number of records you can consult to learn more. A superb website, www.workhouses.org.uk, gives details and locations of different workhouses, information about what conditions were like, including daily routines, punishments, even the food your ancestors might have eaten. Many surviving workhouses have been turned into private houses, hospitals or care homes, but some have also been turned into museums. The aforementioned website has a list of them and they are well worth a visit (www.workhouses.org.uk/visit).

Your local archive or record office should hold the records of any workhouses in that region. There you might be able to find admission and discharge books, registers of baptisms, marriages and deaths inside the workhouse and the records of relieving officers who were charged with interviewing and admitting people or offering 'outdoor relief' in the community, which can offer a poignant glimpse into the personal circumstances of the people they were dealing with.

Old Occupations

On census returns and civil registration certificates you might encounter some occupations that have died out or been renamed. There's a comprehensive database at http://rmhh.co.uk/occup, which is well worth referring to, but here are some common occupations you might come across:

- **ACCOMPTANT:** Accountant.
- **BOILERMAKER:** Trained craftsman who produced plates and sections of steel.
- **COOPER:** Craftsman who made wooden objects such as casks, barrels and buckets.
- **COSTERMONGER:** Fruit and vegetable seller.
- **DRAPER:** Fabric dealer.
- **FOOTMAN:** Male servant.
- **HABERDASHER:** Clothing salesman.
- **HEWER:** Miner who cut ('hewed') coal at the mine face.
- **LAMPLIGHTER:** Employed by the council to light gas street lamps.
- **MILLINER:** Hat maker/seller.
- **MUDLARK:** Someone who made a living scavenging for objects on river banks at low tide.
- **OSTLER:** Employed to look after guests' horses at hotels or inns.

- **SAGGAR MAKER:** Maker of 'saggars', clay kilns in which ceramics were fired (their assistants were called 'bottom knockers').
- **SHIPWRIGHT:** Built or repaired ships.
- **TINKER:** Travelling salesman who sold mainly pots and pans.
- **WEAVER:** Operator of the loom which produced cloth.
- **WHEEL TAPPER:** Railway worker.

December 1910: Some young boys working at the troughs used for cleaning coal at a pit in Bargoed, South Wales.

KATE HUMBLE

As she embarked on a riveting journey into her family's past, TV presenter Kate Humble's only concern was that her ancestors might prove so extraordinary that she would feel as if she had let them down. She had no idea what to expect – all she knew was that both her grandfathers flew. Her maternal grandfather, Stanley Carter, had served in the RAF during the Second World War, while Bill Humble, her paternal grandfather, was a test pilot for Hawker Jets – though, as she admitted, 'I don't really know what that means.'

FROM HER FATHER she learned that Bill was a roguish, raffish character plucked straight from the pages of a *Boy's Own* story. He learned to fly aged 17 and went on to become one of the country's finest demonstration flyers in an era when thousands of people flocked to airfields to watch daredevil pilots perform extraordinary acts of aerial acrobatics. At the outbreak of war he was asked by Hawker to test its new jets before they were used in combat. This was an incredibly dangerous job – one in four test pilots died in accidents. Bill tested the Tempest, his favourite aircraft, which was the only fighter plane capable of keeping up with the deadly Doodlebug bombs that Hitler aimed at London, and which saved hundreds of thousands of lives during the summer of 1944.

* * *

Bill was larger than life. So much so that, in some way, he had ceased to be a grandfather and become a daredevil hero. Kate had been given a recording of a colourful interview with her grandfather, which moved her to tears, tinged with regret that she had not taken the chance to learn about him before.

In that recording, Bill mentioned his training as a mining engineer. His father, William Horsley Humble, had been a colliery owner and Kate wondered how deep the Humble's coal-mining links were. She was surprised to learn that they extended back several generations. Her great-great-great-grandfather, Joseph Humble, had been in charge of a colliery in Northumberland. She travelled

*William Horsley Humble, Kate's
paternal great-grandfather.*

to Woodhorn Colliery, now a museum, to learn more about the
colliery's history and Joseph's working life. In the 1871 census she
learned that Joseph had turned his back on the mining industry and
had become a grocer and draper in Durham.

Why, Kate wondered? She delved deeper and learnt the awful
truth. In 1862 Joseph had been in charge of Hester Pit in Hartley
when the beam of the pit's pumping engine broke and fell down the
shaft, trapping 204 men and boys below – among them, Joseph's
nephew. As there was only one shaft the men had no means of
escape and died a slow, suffocating death in the depths of the mine.

Kate's maternal grandfather,
Stanley Carter.

Newspaper reports spoke of Joseph's grief at the loss of his 'canny men'. As the bodies were brought up and piles of coffins were taken away, he remained steadfastly at his post until the last miner had been recovered. The inquest into what became known as the Hartley Colliery Disaster held no one responsible for the tragic accident, but the grief had taken its toll. Joseph walked away from the industry a heartbroken man.

Kate's focus switched to her maternal grandfather, Stanley Carter. From her mother she learned that Stanley had met and married her grandmother in a whirlwind wartime romance. By the time he was shot down in a bombing raid on Düsseldorf they had known each other only a few months. She asked her mum if he ever spoke of his war service, but like many of his generation, Stanley was not a man to unburden himself, so what happened to him was a mystery. Tantalizingly, she did say he was a renowned 'escaper' and that to stop him the Germans had locked him up in Colditz.

She headed to the National Archives to find out more. It turned out that Stanley had not been in Colditz but Stalag Luft III at the time when 200 men tried to escape through a tunnel, a story immortalized in the film *The Great Escape*. Surviving records suggested that Stanley drew up the maps that the escapees would need as they attempted to make their way across enemy territory and towards safety.

But was he involved in the escape itself? To find out, she travelled to the site of the camp and saw the spot, once Hut 104, where the men had gathered to go down a shaft 30 feet deep to meet a 300-foot tunnel that would take them beyond the perimeter wall. The escape was interrupted when 76 of the men had gone through the tunnel, and there was a good chance Stanley was one of the 124 waiting to

*Circa 1943: The interior of a hut
at Stalag Luft III, where Allied
prisoners of war were imprisoned.*

go. Of the 76 who got out, only three reached freedom; of the 73 that were caught, 50 were summarily executed.

As the Red Army advanced in the winter of 1944/45, Stanley and his fellow prisoners of war were marched hundreds of miles in sub-zero conditions with little food or water for weeks on end. Stanley wrote a vivid diary of the horrific Long March, and Kate followed in his footsteps, visiting many of the places he and his colleagues marched past. Stanley managed to survive; several months and hundreds of miles later he was in Lübeck when it was liberated by British troops. Finally, he could go home to his young wife and the infant daughter he had never seen.

Kate had encountered three remarkable men on her journey. Her concern had proved to be well founded, but rather than being abashed by their fortitude and courage, she was inspired. 'I hope I go through life without being tested like they were,' she said. 'But if I am, I hope I have inherited a shred of their loyalty and bravery.'

EMPIRE WINDRUSH
LONDON

. Date of Arrival 21. 6.

Whence Arrived TRINIDAD, KINGST
HAVANA, BERMUDA.

PASSENGERS.

	(7)	(8)
dress ingdom	Profession, Occupation, or Calling of Passengers	Country of last Permanent Residence *
cy- sheroe.	Planter.	Trinidad.
Scholars.	H.D.	"
.W.l. orres.	Student.	"
Gdns. lx, ibridge	H.D.	British Guiana.
	Bank Clerk.	"
rdeen.	H.D.	England.
	"	Trinidad.
s, e.	Merchant.	"
	Agriculturalist.	Uganda.
l.	H.D.	England.
	" Master Mariner.	St.Lucia. Trinidad.
.W.7. Gdns.	H.D.	"
s.	Civil Servant.	England. Trinidad.
.l.	"	"
ibridge. ny St,	Student. Civil Servant.	England. Trinidad.
	H.D.	"
choplers. .W.l.	Audit Clerk. Student.	" "
ion. rset, ad.	Spinster. Agricultural Officer.	" Kenya Colony.
	H.D.	Trinidad.
•	Cable Clerk.	"
	Judge.	British Guiana.
.London.	H.D. Civil Servant.	"
	H.D.	"
	-	
	Spinster.	England.
Rd,	H.D.	Trinidad.
£ rtown o.	Retired. Student.	England. N.Ireland.
	Dressmaker.	Trinidad.
ring. mue.	Joiner. Medical.	England. "
	H.D.	"
l, and.	Student.	Scotland.
ester.	Telegraphy.	Trinidad.
	H.D.	"
	Student.	"
	"	

IMMIGRANTS
AND EXPATS

IMMIGRANTS AND EXPATS

With a few exceptions, the British have always been a welcoming group. Despite recent hysterical newspaper reports warning of 'floods' of immigrants coming to despoil our green and pleasant land, the truth is that migrants have made their way here for centuries, either fleeing from war and persecution or looking for a better life for themselves and their families. Many of us will encounter migrant ancestors as we journey through our family's past, uncovering some fascinating and moving stories in the process.

***

In fact, our attitude towards immigrants was so liberal that before the nineteenth century it is relatively difficult to track our immigrant ancestors. Unlike other nations, we didn't ask those coming here to register on arrival. There is no equivalent to the United States' Ellis Island, where new arrivals were processed and checked – but this means a scant paper trail for us. The first clue our immigrant ancestors might leave is on a census return, stating their place of birth. So how do you go about researching them?

Let's take the 1851 census, for example. It reveals that almost a quarter of Liverpool's population was born in Ireland. Why so many? To understand this, and most other immigration stories, it's worth trying to learn what was happening in the world at the time, particularly in the place of your ancestor's birth. In this case, Ireland was ravaged by the Great Famine. Men, women and children were starving and left their homeland in search of work, food and survival. Liverpool is just a short journey across the Irish Sea, so it

Jamaican immigrants on board the ex-troopship,
Empire Windrush at Tilbury, 1948.

became the most popular port. Other groups who came to England
in the nineteenth century include Jews fleeing the pogroms of the
Russian Empire in the later decades, and Germans escaping the
upheavals in their homeland during the middle of the century.

The best starting point in your search for any immigrant
ancestors is within your family. They might be able to provide
you with the background details you need to further your search.
There might also be some documents, diaries, letters, or even
something as a precious as a ticket or boarding pass to identify
how they reached these shores. The actor David Suchet always
suspected that his father's line had Eastern European origins. His
older brother John told him that their father, Jack, had once opened
up to him, explaining that the family had changed their name to
Suchet when they were living in South Africa. He remembered his

father said he originally came from small town in Lithuania, then part of East Prussia.

David then turned to his extended family in South Africa for more help. This is another excellent research path to follow. Email and Skype have made the world a much smaller place, and contacting distant relatives in far-off lands has never been easier or cheaper. David learned that his great-grandparents were called Jacob and Beila Suchedowitz – the family name until his father changed it, which gave him the information he needed to start unravelling the mystery of where his father's family originated.

So the rule is: start at home, gather as much information as you can and then look at birth, marriage and death certificates and census returns to try and pinpoint the moment your ancestor arrived in this country. Then a good source of information is the passenger lists from 1878 to 1960 (although many pre-1890 were destroyed). These are available online at www.ancestry.co.uk. For further information, it is also worth consulting the National Archives' online guide to other immigrant records in its collection at www.nationalarchives.gov.uk/records/looking-for-person/immigrants.htm.

Another useful resource for family historians are denization and naturalization records. After arriving, if they wished to become British citizens, migrants had two choices: naturalization, which offered more rights but was more expensive, or denization, which many people chose because it was cheaper, even though it meant they had no right to vote. But there were also many immigrants who chose neither option and never became British citizens. For those who did, the records are at the National Archives. You can find more information and search naturalization case papers online

at www.nationalarchives.gov.uk/records/looking-for-person/
naturalised-britons.htm.

Jewish Ancestry

The website www.jewishgen.org has free, easy-to-use databases
that can help your research, sourced from across the world. There's
also the opportunity to link up with other family researchers who
might have researched the same information you're looking for,
and a discussion group where you can ask questions, swap tips and
focus on specific geographic areas. It's also worth visiting the Jewish
Genealogical Society of Great Britain's website (www.jgsgb.org.uk).

Afro-Caribbean and Indian Ancestors

The years between 1948 and 1962 saw an increase in immigration
from Commonwealth countries, in part to address the labour
shortage after the Second World War and the desire of migrants to
seek a better quality of life. There were few restrictions in that period
and the vast majority of migrants came from the Caribbean and the
Indian sub-continent. People like athlete Colin Jackson's grandfather,
who left Jamaica for the cold of Cardiff in 1955 in search of work. He
brought his children with him, but left his wife, Maria, behind so
she could nurse her sick father while he raised his children single-
handedly in a strange country.

Quality and access to records can vary by country, so for first-,
second- and third-generation immigrants it is crucial to speak to
your family and learn as much as possible from them if you can.
There are few available records from 1960 onwards. From those who
journeyed here, their relatives and friends, even the people they left
behind back home, you will be able to learn about their stories and
uncover further avenues for research, as well as find vital documents
and memorabilia. For more stories, case histories and background,

as well as valuable advice on tracing your roots, consult www. movinghere.org.uk (it also has information about Jewish and Irish as well as Caribbean and South Asian migrants). Sadly, since 2013, the website is no longer being updated but it remains a wonderful resource for those in search of their   immigrant roots.

For those tracing their roots in the West Indies, the National Archives has Colonial Office Records, copies of censuses taken in the West Indies, military records, government gazettes, wills, court cases, registers of slaves, and much more. An excellent place to start is the *Tracing Your Caribbean Ancestors* by Guy Grannum (Bloomsbury, 2012).

Tracing Your British Indian Ancestors by Emma Jolly (Pen & Sword Family History, 2012) is a good launching pad for those seeking to find more about their Indian roots. It gives an exhaustive guide to the resources you can find in various archives. How far back you'll be able to trace your family ancestry in India depends on several factors: how much information you have about your family origins and your family's religious denomination. It's unlikely you'll be able to find any information online, although it's always worth trying www.familysearch.org.

Emigrants and Expats

Just as immigrants have been making this country their home for centuries, so people have emigrated in search of new lives elsewhere. In the nineteenth century alone it's estimated that ten million people left Britain. The most popular destinations were the United States and the new-found colonies, including Canada and Australia. The ancestors of Jodie Kidd were among the early settlers in New England, while Jason Donovan's forebears took a less voluntary route to Australia...

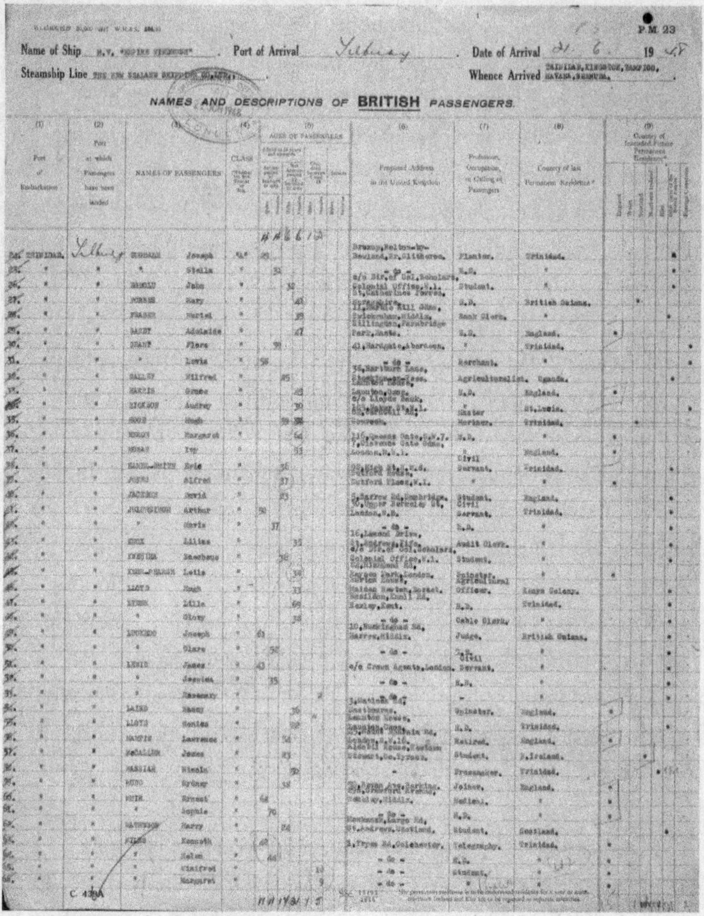
P.M. 23

Name of Ship M.V. "EMPIRE WINDRUSH". Port of Arrival Tilbury. Date of Arrival 21. 6. 1948

Steamship Line THE NEW ZEALAND SHIPPING CO. LTD. Whence Arrived TRINIDAD, KINGSTON, TAMPICO, HAVANA, BERMUDA.

NAMES AND DESCRIPTIONS OF **BRITISH** PASSENGERS.

(1) Port of Embarkation	(2) Port at which Passengers have been landed	(3) Names of Passengers	(4) Class	(5) Ages of Passengers	(6) Proposed Address in the United Kingdom	(7) Profession, Occupation, or Calling of Passengers	(8) Country of last Permanent Residence*	(9) Country of Intended Future Permanent Residence*

Passenger list for the SS Empire Windrush, 1948.

The best place to start your search for emigrant ancestors is in the country they chose as their new home. For example, if they emigrated to the United States they might have passed through and been processed at Ellis Island, and you can search for their names on the database www.ellisisland.org, which covers the period between 1892 and 1924. The website ancestry.co.uk has a number of US passenger lists, all fully searchable by name. Closer to home, findmypast.co.uk has a database of outbound passenger lists from the UK between 1890 and 1960.

Our ancestors might also have lived and worked abroad, perhaps for the British Empire in one of its colonies. The impressionist and comedian Alistair McGowan was always curious about his family's bloodline, in particular whether there was any Indian ancestry in the mix. Research revealed that generations of McGowans had been born in India, working for the Raj and the East India Company, dating back to 1775. With the assistance of a local historian, Alistair found a reference to a gloriously named ancestor, Suetonius McGowan. He learned that Suetonius married a noble Muslim lady, whose name was omitted from the baptism record because she refused to convert to Christianity. The mystery was solved: here was the Indian link that Alistair McGowan suspected he would find.

The British Library is the custodian of the records of baptisms, marriages and burials of those who worked in the East India Company or the India Office. The African and Asian Studies Reading Room there holds the largest UK-based collection of India Office Records. Alongside this collection researchers can also look for their ancestors among church, company and civil records. Guidance can be find on the British Library's 'India Office Family History' webpage. Many of these records are now available to search online at findmypast.co.uk, along with millions of other military and civil records, including pensions and wills.

*Immigrants from Jamaica arrive at Tilbury, London,
on board the empire Windrush, 1948. The party are
five young boxers and their manager.*

NITIN GANATRA

EastEnders star Nitin Ganatra had always felt rootless. He moved to England from Kenya with his family when he was only three years old and had never felt a sense of belonging in his new home. The main aim of his journey was to fill in the many gaps in his past and pass his history on to his sons as a gift, hopefully giving them a sense of 'home' he had never experienced.

HE WENT BACK to visit his parents in the shop his father bought only a few weeks after swapping the sun-kissed plains of Kenya for the rain-drenched concrete of Coventry. In a revealing conversation with them, he learnt a host of things he had never known: that his father had left Kenya penniless and had only been able to borrow the money to open a shop after offering his wife's jewellery as surety; that his grandfather had left India to be a labourer on the railways in Kenya; and, most startling of all, that his maternal grandparents had married when his grandmother was six and his grandfather ten.

* * *

From Coventry he flew to Nairobi to investigate the life of his great-grandfather, Popatlal. He was one of 32,000 Gujarati workers who built the trans-Kenyan railway. It was backbreaking, dangerous work: 2,500 men died and 7,000 more were invalided back to India. Popatlal survived and, rather than returning to his homeland, chose to forge a new life for his family in Kenya. He settled in a new town, Broderick Falls, built beside the railway he had just helped to construct, and brought his family over. They built a flourishing family business, which was inherited by Nitin's father, Jayantilal, in the 1950s. Nitin visited his father's old store and learned why his father chose to leave. After gaining independence in 1963, Kenya's leaders pushed policies to promote native Africans in business and education. The Indian community were encouraged to take Kenyan citizenship. By 1967, new laws were passed limiting trade for those who weren't citizens. Jhantilal faced a tough decision:

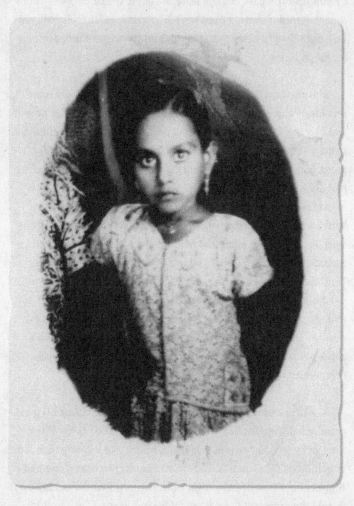

*Nitin's mother, Manglaben,
as a child.*

take citizenship and keep his business, or keep hold of his British Commonwealth passport and leave. He chose the latter option, even though it meant starting from scratch in a strange land. He believed England offered a better home for his family and greater opportunity for his children.

The next stop on Nitin's journey was Rajkot in India. There he met his mother's sister, who told him that their father had become ill and that she and Nitin's mother had been forced to work as children to help support the family. But that wasn't the only hardship they faced. Nitin learned that they had eight brothers and sisters who had died. He set off to learn more about this shocking fact. Child mortality rates were falling in India in the mid-twentieth century. Why had so many of them died? Unfortunately, very few records exist. People died at home and their relatives felt no need to register their deaths. Miraculously, the death of one of Nitin's dead aunts, Dudhiben, had been recorded. She was six years old. The cause of death was 'fever' but Nitin was told that it was likely she had died of malaria. There was another possible factor in her and her siblings' deaths – their mother's age when she gave birth. As she was still a child, perhaps just 13 or 14, it was possible the children had been born underweight and unable to survive.

The next step on Nitin's journey was Jharera, the village his great-grandfather, Popatlal, left to live in Kenya. No record exists of that time, but the oldest man in the village, believed to be more than 100, remembered the Ganatras. They owned land, grew cotton and had a shop selling a type of palm sugar called jaggery. Remembering how he told the camera at the start about his rootlessness, an emotional Nitin spoke of how it felt to visit his ancestral home: 'It's good to call somewhere home, isn't it?'

Nitin as a child (circled).

The final leg of his epic journey was to Mathura, the birthplace of Krishna and a holy city that attracts pilgrims from all across India and the world. There, a high priest had kept records of all the Ganatras who had visited the city over centuries. To his astonishment, Nitin was able to learn of his ancestors going back nine generations. But that wasn't the only surprise. He had forgotten that, when he was eight, he had visited Mathura with his father. He saw his name written in the family's book. He was able to add the names of his sons to his family's history: a very proud moment.

At the conclusion of his story, Nitin had found his sense of belonging. It wasn't to a place, but to a family. Understanding its story had helped him understand his feelings and achieve a sense of peace. 'I can be in India now and relax; I can be in Kenya and relax; I can be in England and relax,' he said. 'The answer isn't in one place. What is mine and my family's is my tribe – I belong to that tribe.'

JASON DONOVAN

In terms of family history, singer Jason Donovan has always felt a greater connection with the UK than his native Australia. His father, the actor Terence Donovan, was English-born and has told his son of the family's west London roots, while his wife and two children are English. He was less sure of his Australian identity and his maternal family history. His father and mother separated when he was young; he lived with his father and is estranged from his mother, Sue Menlove. 'Maybe looking into this now will give me a better understanding of her life because it's a pretty blank canvas, unfortunately,' he told the camera.

HE TRAVELLED to Melbourne, the city where he grew up, to meet his father, who showed him a batch of documents his maternal grandmother, Joan Dawson, had given to him. Her mother, Eileen Dawson, had been a singer, although the details of her career were unclear. Jason visited his cousin Judy McCardy, Eileen's granddaughter, to find out more. He discovered that Eileen Lyons, as she was before marriage, had entered show business aged 17, encouraged by her father, Simeon. Judy told Jason that Eileen rarely spoke about her career in later life and the newspaper clippings she collected ended around 1915, when she was still a young woman.

* * *

More research revealed that Eileen had been contracted to K. C. Williamson, a sort of early Australian Andrew Lloyd Webber, but also earned success performing vaudeville with another well-known impresario, Harry Rickards. She must have been very talented, but her career was brought to an abrupt halt when she married Horace Dawson, a flamboyant pool hall manager, and had children. The rest of her life was devoted to them, and later her grandchildren, although an internal ABC memo from 1941 revealed that she tried to make a comeback aged 55, but it's unclear how that ended. Eileen died in 1976, and Jason wondered if her entertainment experiences influenced his mother's decision to enter show business.

Next on his research list was Simeon Lyons, Eileen's father. From his birth certificate Jason learned that he was born in Tasmania, so

*Eileen Lyons, Jason's maternal
great-grandmother.*

he travelled to Hobart to find out more. In the Tasmanian Convict
Index he found an entry for Joseph Lyons, Simeon's father, who
had been found guilty at the Old Bailey of receiving stolen goods
and sentenced to ten years in a penal colony. His wife, Rosetta, had
been tried alongside him and found not guilty. Jason discovered
that the couple had lived in Whitechapel in the heart of the Jewish
community until this sentence ripped the family apart.

It was the height of transportation. Officially, convicts were
sent to Australia because of overflowing prisons in the UK, but
unofficially the new colony was in dire need of free labour to exploit
its abundant natural resources. Joseph spent the first few years of his

*Jason as a child (top right) with
his actor father, Terence Donovan,
(right) and estranged mother,
Sue Menlove (left).*

sentence working on a road gang by day and locked in a dingy cell
by night. Remarkably, and unusually, Rosetta had sailed out to be
with him three years after he had been sentenced. Joseph had been
released on probation, taken in by a Jewish family in Tasmania and
had either earned the money to reunite his family or been given it by
his benefactors. He was eventually granted his freedom but returned
to Whitechapel and his native London in 1856, although Simeon,
who had been born in Australia, went back to the country in his
twenties and settled there for good.

Buoyed by this knowledge, Jason wanted go even further back
into his maternal line. With the help of the Society of Genealogists,

he managed to trace his Australian heritage back seven generations to a man named William Cox. William had also travelled to Australia in its penal colony days, but in direct contrast to Joseph Lyons, he was a soldier in charge of convicts rather than one of their number.

William was an enterprising man who soon took full advantage of the opportunities in New South Wales, growing a large agricultural holding with the help of convict labour, whom he always treated fairly and with respect. Australia at that stage was only New South Wales. The rest of the country remained unexplored and unexploited. Those settlers in Sydney were hemmed in by the Blue Mountains, unable to access the arable land beyond. A severe drought had caused a crisis in food supply and a road through the mountains was essential for the colony's future. The man charged with building that 101-mile road was William Cox.

Jason was left astonished by the scale of the undertaking – 'man against nature' as he described it. The narrowest point across the range still meant hacking through forest and cutting through sheer cliff-faces made of sandstone and granite. All Cox's 30 convict labourers had for the task were pickaxes, shovels and gunpowder and, at one point, they were presented with a sheer drop of 1,000 feet. Yet Cox and his men were able to build the road in only six months – more than six times faster than had been estimated. It was a remarkable achievement. Providing settlers with access to the interior, William had ensured that a struggling penal colony could transform itself into a thriving nation. As a consequence, Jason felt 'very proud' to be an Australian. 'I'm glad I've touched base with the Australian in me, which, I have to say, originates from my mother,' he said at the end of his journey. 'That's a good thing.'

INDEX

ACKNOWLEDGEMENTS

This book could not have been written without the help of a number of people. In no particular order: Alex Graham, for giving up his time to talk about the show's origins; Kathryn Taylor and the team at Wall to Wall for sharing their material and going over the manuscript in such fine detail; Anna Kirkwood, who prepared the case study of Billy Connolly's programme; the BBC Commissioning Executive Maxine Watson; and Sara Kahn and Laura Berry, who's keen genealogical eyes weeded out any mistakes and omissions. Thanks to you all.

At BBC books and Random House, I'd like to thank my editor Lorna Russell and Louise McKeever for their support and expertise. Finally, hearty cheers and thanks to Julian Alexander and the wonderful team at LAW for all their encouragement and help.

Picture credits: © Adrian Kerton 15; © Alamy 34, 48, 56, 78, 84, 95, 97; © Angus and Virginia Armstrong 101, 102; © Diana Humble 163, 164; © Diana Janus 76 (two images); © Erica Gross 31; © Evelyn Strauch 33; © Getty Images 6, 10, 18, 22, 40, 42, 106, 122, 148, 153, 155, 156, 159, 166, 168, 177; © Judy McArd 187; © Linda Ayton 147; © Maglaben Ganatra 181; © Marcianne Harriott-Harris 120; © Mary Cumming 139, 141; © Nitin Ganatra 183; © Oscar Harriott 121; © Terence Donovan 188; © Topfoto 6, 34, 38, 54, 56, 60, 62, 78, 87, 93, 106, 111, 115, 122, 128, 130, 132, 148, 168, 171, 175; © Trevor Stewart 145; © Wall To Wall Media Limited/Photographer: Andrew Montgomery 28, 50, 72, 98, 116, 136, 142, 160, 184; © Wall To Wall Media Limited/Photographer: Ed Miller 178.